FREE TO FLY:

Wisdom for the Seasons in a Woman's Life

FREE TO FLY:

Wisdom for the Seasons in a Woman's Life

A Collection of Writing Compiled and Edited by
Penda L. James

InSCRIBEd Inspiration, LLC.
Pittsburgh, PA 15221

Free to Fly: Wisdom for the Seasons in a Woman's Life
Published by InSCRIBEd Inspiration

Cover Design: Lauren Lake
Layout: Just Ink Digital Design
Photography: Stephanie Davis

Library of Congress Control Number: 2009910229
ISBN 13: 978-0-9792385-2-9
ISBN 10: 0-9792385-2-8

Dedication to our loved ones:

A Haiku

No longer broken
We now find restoration
Teaching you to fly . . .

Contents

From the Editor 1
The Beauty of a Woman Is 4

BROKEN WINGS:
The Season of Brokenness

The Strength of a Woman . . . Coni Hookfin 6
Taken in the Night/P.A.I.N Catt4297 8
Broken to Be Free Shantal "Peaches" Cabell .. 9
Quit or Get Stronger Valerie D. Jones 11
Lonely Teryn Aliya Barker 16
Brokenness Lynette Michelle Mashiri 17
I Killed My Best Friend's Babies
     Tina Renee McKinney 18
Ripples of Anger, I Denise Thomas 25
Babe's Heart Still Bleeds Teisha Durham 27
The Funeral Judi Gazaway 33
My Testimony Selener Fields 34

Gathering the Wisdom from Broken Wings 35

FEAR OF FALLING:
The Season of Nurturing

Gather Enough for Today Nicole Colvin 39
A Child of Our Own Teri Miller Barker 40
Babylon Burning @ Her Back,
     Canto I, Canto II Avalyn*Abijah* 47
Testimony on Obedience Tanika M. Carwile 51
Appreciate What You Got Sylvia Jewett 53

A Prayer of Petition   Maya D. Green................ 56
Silent Tears of Hope and Joy
      Marilyn J.P. Horton............................ 59
A Precious Gift   Robin Taylor............................ 62
Freudian Slip   Sierra Leone............................... 65
Stepdad   Theresa Burrage...................................... 68
Pleasures of Life Diane   I. Daniels 69
Hear My Cry O' Lord   LaShonda B. Fuller......... 78
On Top of the World   Penda L. James 80

Gathering the Wisdom from Fear of Falling......... 97

LEARNING TO SOAR:
The Season of Maturity

My Mama Used to Say TyRhonda Coleman...... 101
Preference (For Jean Gray)   Sierra Leone........ 102
For My Daughter   Teri Miller Barker 104
The Mirror Called My Daughter
      Ebony Broussard 105
What I Know   Annie M. Wright Jones.............. 108
Untitled   Shanna Owens 111
Testimony I, Testimony II   Kristin Young......... 112
Reconnecting with   Gwendolyn D. Buchanan ... 114
Spirit   LaFlora Sholar 117
Latte and Lorna Doones   Danada Beckwith....... 119
That's What I'll Do   uNique............................ 124
New Beginnings   Myra Michele George............. 126
Trusting God's Direction When There
     is No Direction Lauren Lake 130
Sigh Lizbeth Figueroa Marino 138
Prayer or Prozac? Stephanie Davis.................... 139
I Realize Karasimone Pennybaker 146
I AM   Kenya Arnold.. 147

For Ruth   Joyce Nelson 148

Gathering the Wisdom from Learning to Soar 150

FREE TO FLY:
The Season of Freedom

Untitled   Christine Arnett................................. 154
Be!   Paisha Thomas.. 155
Back to Beautiful   Penda L. James 157
Our Mothers   Theresa Burrage 159
Soar   Jaquan Johnson 160
A Glimpse into my Soul
    Charlene A. Hill-Ellison 162
Phoenix/Uprising   Yolanda McElroy................. 166
The Sign in my Shop Window!
    Orienta Nicole Eison..................................... 168
Masquerade   Marla Holloway........................... 171
Free to Fly   Alvina D. Smith............................. 174
Who Am I?   LaShonda B. Fuller....................... 176
A New Day   Tiwanda Alston............................. 178
The Season of Me   Lena Arnold...................... 183
My Legacy   Lyndell O. Robinson...................... 189
Babylon Burning @ Her Back, Canto III
    Avalyn*Abijah* 192
Housewarming   Mariama Whyte...................... 194
Dandelion Bouquets   Penda L. James.............. 214

Gathering the Wisdom from Free to Fly 223

The Strength of a Woman is 225
The Contributors.. 226
About the Editor 237
Acknowledgements 238

"Baby, I didn't know. . ."

"Baby, I didn't know that I needed to talk to you about your shape so that I could protect you." My mother was telling me about her client whose body looked like an adult woman, but she was only fourteen.

I still remember the look on my mom's face – the deep pain in her eyes, the flow of her tears, and the quiver in her voice, "She was raped."

I had been sexually abused. Unbeknownst to me, my mother carried the burden of my violation for years – she felt that she did not protect me. I knew how the young girl would fight to love herself and her forthcoming internal battles against confusion, anger and sadness.

"I was never curvaceous, but what I learned today is that men are attracted to a particular body type. You have that body type. . . I didn't." My mother's ruminations were eye opening, "men were not attracted to me in the same way they look at you. What bothers me most," she continued, "you didn't tell me someone was hurting you."

I had been intentional for years about keeping things from her. I knew some of my mother's struggles. I didn't want to add to her burdens. I watched my mother and because I didn't now her internal strength I judged what I saw in her actions as weakness. "I resented you for a long time," I admitted to my mother. "I thought I was watching you deteriorate from a woman of poise, strength and confidence into someone who didn't care about herself. . . that angered me." I never asked her any questions; I only made decisions from my assumptions.

On bad days I walked into my closet with my boom box, closed the door and sang out loud in the darkness. In that closet, I prayed, cried and bandaged my wounds with food. I yearned for release of my secrets, but I was too afraid to talk about them, too ashamed to tell the truth and too immature to ask for help.

"Yes, I had struggles, but I am still your mother and I have a responsibility for you. You took that from me when you kept your silence. You told me when I couldn't help you and I am so sorry that happened to you."

That conversation helped my mother and I break down walls. Our bond was strengthened as the lines of our communication were opened. I just hate that I had a fear of falling for thirty-two years.

The purpose of this book is to expose some of the taboo subjects (death, sex, suicide, our fathers, organ donation, low self-esteem, feminism, and growing older) and encourage women to be deliberate in contemplating them aloud. Through these poems, short stories, testimonies and statements of faith, it is my hope that healing circles will be formed, broken relationships will be restored and lives will be rededicated to faith. Ultimately, bandaged wounds which have been ignored will be healed and freedom will be embraced.

Young women like Catt4297 and Teryn Barker have a story that needs to be heard. For them let us be honest about out lives and verbalize our mistakes and accomplishments so we can pass wisdom forward. Through these exchanges we will all be able to walk with confidence and poise into our destiny knowing that we are in the Master's hands.

Inspired to find my freedom,

Penda Lynn James

"Come with me my sistahs and help me heal."
Deborah Y. Pendleton

The beauty of a woman is

. . .

Indefinable.
Judi Gazaway

her freedom to nurture.
Edwin Dunn

her love for God.
Hubie Pitts

her strength.
Erica Lyn Williams

her belief that she can fly anywhere she wants to go.
Elna Horton

her song in the dark.
Penda L. James

BROKEN WINGS:
The Season of Brokenness

Broken Wings represent events in our lives that tear us apart, break our spirit and cause us great pain. We ask questions like, "Where is God? Does He still love me? Why is *this* happening to *me*?"

At the time, we don't realize that brokenness is a temporary season — it feels like eternity so we tear our hair out in stress at the thought of our dreams being crushed, kick ourselves for allowing our spirit to be shaken, shut ourselves off from others to prevent our emotions from being bruised again.

Coni Hookfin

THE STRENGTH
OF A WOMAN . . .

Is determined by many things – sex, money and
men
just to name a few.
Education, children and peace of mind are mine
. . .
What about you?

He told me when we first met,
"You mean more to me than life itself."
With those same lips he forced me to lie to
myself.
. . . *to thine own self be true*?

My struggle lies in how I could be true
When I loved you but didn't like you.

My heart was shattered, mind fragmented,
my being damaged — who could have loved me
the way that I was packaged?

. . . I <u>chose</u> to live this life under the label of a
wife.
Such a shame, such a shame.
I didn't like me but who was really to blame?

Such indecision made my insides die
Lord please lead me to the Rock that is higher
than I.

Catt4297
(Age 11)

TAKEN IN THE NIGHT

Taken in the night
My dream, my hope

Taken in the night
My heart is what you broke

Taken in the night
My happiness, my laugh

Taken in the night
My body, which was torn in half

Taken in the night
My ambitions, my innocence

The time I never cried again

P.A.I.N.

P Possibilities that you took

A Ambitions you took from me

I Incredible pain you caused

N Negativity you brought me

Shantal "Peaches" Cabell

BROKEN TO BE FREE

GOD is it you to help me break the chains
holding me from so many things that i allow to
break me?

The things i feel often make my head spin and
hurt. . .
what causes it?
what makes my heart hurt for things i want to
push away,
people i could never push away and have to
love,
people i want to let go but can't because i fear
the unknown

wanting more, too broken to release myself and
persevere for more . . .

Where is my faith and why can't i let Him take
over?
because i can't be free to change
my past abuse, hurts, aches, pains, and wounds
i try to let go, but they come back to haunt the
person inside who wants to be free

i keep holding them in smiling; claiming to be
free; laughing, claiming to be me;
crying, praying, and hoping it will all be alright

the pain in my soul engulfs me, it overcomes me
with grief
a whirlwind of emotions bottled up inside with
no one to share them with . . . how can i free
myself?
the pain in my head is it an aneurysm waiting to
happen
do i always speak bad over my life? — no.

i am a new creature . . . people don't understand.
. .
they only see what i portray and that is not
always me. . .
i am a woman of standards and love,
compassion and dreams . . .

Valerie D. Jones

QUIT OR GET STRONGER

*When everything relative to your life seems to
be broken in a million pieces, don't trust
yourself to fit the pieces,
but look to the one who is a mastermind
at putting broken pieces back together again.*

No matter where we find ourselves in life, we all will face a season of brokenness. It is never meant to destroy us, but to make us realize that no man is self-sufficient without God's help. Brokenness can be seen as a "new beginning." There will be things that come against us that we will be able to breeze through feeling no pain, but then there are those seasons when everything you know to do isn't enough.

My saga began twenty five years ago. I was married and had two daughters who were the apples of my eye. My husband at the time was a truck driver and I was a government employee when those great words "you're pregnant," were spoken. You can only imagine the joy everyone felt with the thought of a boy being born into a family dominated by girls.

After a full term of carrying him, out came my nine pound bouncing baby boy. I will be the first to admit I was on top of the world.

Three years later I found myself pregnant again, only this time things weren't the same. For seven months I could keep nothing down and for some reason I felt that something was not quite right. After twenty three hours of labor my second son was born. He was jaundiced and weighed five pounds fifteen ounces. I remember being released from the hospital, unaware that his hospital days had only begun.

After a checkup and blood work I was informed by the doctor that not one, but both of my sons had been diagnosed with Sickle Cell Disease — I was devastated. That day I left the doctor's office feeling like the weight of the world had been dumped on my shoulders. My husband's addiction to alcohol made him abusive and caused our marriage to end. I was alone with four children, two who had been diagnosed with a devastating disease.

I remember saying to myself, "Why me? Why me? What am I going to do?" while trying to hold back tears.

Brokenness has a way of making you quit or making you stronger. I guess for me the latter carried the heavier weight. I must inject though, that after more than 10 years of everything except peace, brokenness took its toll on me. Mentally I was a wreck, physically I was worn, and emotionally I had more days of crying than smiling. Unbeknownst to my family and friends I wished I were dead. All I wanted was rest but I needed peace even more.

Being sole provider for my family was taxing. I had to work extra hard, sometimes two jobs to make ends meet. My oldest daughter had to step into a place not designed for any twelve-year old. My car was barely drivable and because he was being paid under the table, we had no child support. There were doctor visits, Sickle Cell crises and long stays in the hospital. I was bathing and running from the hospital trying to make sure my girls were getting to school on time. There was the stress of getting to work on time, and on top of everything else, meeting doctors at the hospital who always seemed to say something I didn't want to hear.

It was a continual nightmare. I kept hoping to go to sleep and wake up to everything back to normal. Every time I thought things were getting better they had gotten worse. There were sleepless nights because of my son's pain; machines going off, and nurses in and out of the rooms. I only had a few people who could help me. After awhile, even family got tired because of their own obligations, and no matter how much they may have wanted to help, I was usually alone.

It was my responsibility to make sure my son was safe and not afraid when he was in the hospital. I couldn't imagine that he would wake up and I was not there for him. One night while I sat with my son I couldn't sleep. At around 3:00 in the morning I realized I had no one to turn to, and no place to go, so I opened my Bible. God took me to Isaiah 43:2:

> *"When you pass through the waters, I will be with you; And through the rivers, they shall not overflow you. When you walk through the fire, you shall not be burned, Nor shall the flame scorch you. (NKJV)"*

I tried to hold back tears that kept coming. I read the scripture until I felt better. The love and warmth of my Heavenly Father penetrated my being. For the first time in a long while, I didn't have fear. I began to feel the peace I so desperately needed. My tired, worn and broken body was able to drift off to sleep as I awaited the results of more tests.

Thinking back to that time, I can admit how difficult it was. The blessing is that both of my boys are fine now. My older son has not had any attacks since he was thirteen. I believe he is healed! My younger son rarely has an attack; in the past four years he's only been hospitalized three times, and to me that's a blessing.

Sometimes it's impossible to see the good of being broken. Think about Jesus when His hour of brokenness came in the Garden of Gethsemane; He had to rely on a higher power, the only power that would be able to get Him through the most difficult time of His life. Wind, storms, and rain have their place in our lives but rest assured, at some point calm will come.

Teryn Aliya Barker
(Age 10)

LONELY

I miss you.
I think of you here and there.
I know you think I might not care,
But in my eyes lie a lonely stare.
So far away I have to say,
When I think of you,
The clouds turn gray.
You were my best friend,
And now my heart just won't mend.
The stars, the moon,
The ground, the sky,
Feel bad for me,
They want to cry.
I hope you are okay,
And don't feel bad.
Too late for me,
I'm already sad!

Lynette Michelle Mashiri

BROKENNESS

I thought I was whole,
Complete,
the total woman

"Not so," said the Lord,
"You may be a grown woman
But still a child you are to me."
So, starting with the inside
He broke me up.
All the things I held dear
Old friends, habits,
He took them all
Deeper, inside, all that baggage
And I thought I was done
"Not yet," He said,
"More needs to go
I am the Potter and you are the clay
Let me mold me you to be the woman I called
you to be."
So naked and unashamed I am, broken to a
stump so
He can make me more whole in Him
And it's only when we surrender to being
broken by Him
He can build us up

Surrender to brokenness

Tina Renee McKinney

I KILLED MY BEST FRIEND'S BABIES

Adults never talked to us about *it*. The most my mother ever said was, "Keep your dress down and your panties up." Like that would be enough for a generation of kids who grew up watching their older aunts and uncles burn bras, smoke marijuana, shack up and sex up. We were a generation who grew up hearing our favorite idols say sex was okay, especially if you "loved somebody." We listened to a boatload of music that talked about sex and not to mention that we were watching it in the movies they often took us to see. "Keep your dress down and your panties up," was enough for her generation, but it wasn't nearly enough for mine. We needed something more, but we never got it.

There we were two seniors, eighteen year old virgins and as far as we knew, the only ones left. We thought we knew it all as most seniors do, discussing sex-related issues. Each day before school we'd meet on the school bus, after a night of hanging out with our boyfriends, (both captains on the football team), and before our butts could reach the seat we're asking each other, "Did you do *it* yet?" As if *it* was something as simple as climbing a tree or jumping a fence. That was about the extent of our conversation on sex. Yes, like most of us naïve teens, we yielded to the belief that *everyone was doing it.*

This was the eighties, long before the popularity of prevention programs and long before any of us ever heard about AIDS.

We never understood that each time we asked each other the question our resolve to stay pure was growing weaker. Each one of us never really recognized that the other was looking for a reason to say no; but we never gave each other that reason.

We'd become too brainwashed by the media. Movies, television, music, each bombarded us daily with lustful messages, and we, all grown up, did not want to appear to be CHILDREN. So, our brains, weary from the battle on all fronts, simply shut down. Our friends were doing *it*, our boyfriends wanted *it* and our heroes sanctioned *it*! What could we do but give in? Besides, there didn't seem to be any "real" harm.

And so, armed with our warped sense of values, we made plans to give away our virginity. We planned it for prom night since it was a few weeks after our eighteenth birthdays. We wanted to officially wait until we were eighteen as if that made it more "special." We fancied ourselves to be superior to our friends who had lost theirs at fourteen and fifteen. I use the term lost it loosely. For no one can really lose something if they know where it is. Unless, they never knew how valuable what they had was. So I guess in effect they did not lose it; just like we had not. We were so smart she and I — at least that's what we thought. In reality we were simply used.

Don't misunderstand me; these were not bad guys in the traditional sense of bad guys. But they were guys, filled with youthful ignorance and raging hormones. Like us their lives were filled with many bad role models, and few wise counselors. Besides, it wasn't their responsibility to keep our legs closed. It was ours.

The consequences of our actions were immediate. We became confused at the loss of our innocence. We were no longer special. We became just like the others: statistics in somebody's social services report. We lost the joy of our senior year as we entered into "mini marriages." Jealousy issues began to arise, struggles for control became a problem, and complicated choices regarding pregnancy had to be made.

As we struggled with these issues, bitterness which led to anger, which led to violence, began to creep in. Fun was replaced by fear. Fear of pregnancy, fear our parents would find out, fear of jealous rages, fear of the future and fear of each other. The worst part is, the things we should have feared the most we didn't, like sexually transmitted diseases.

If only I had recognized how valuable I was as a person. If only someone had said to me as Solomon said to the women of Israel, *"I charge you O' Daughters of Jerusalem . . . do not stir up or awaken love until it pleases."* If only I had realized that my virginity was a gift from God. A precious jewel. A jewel that I'd like to be able to say I gave to the highest bidder, but that would be a lie. The highest bidder would have been the one willing to wait until we were both old enough to understand true love and commitment.

I'm not really sure why I did it. I'd held out for so long. I wasn't even all that interested. He just kept pushing me and pressuring me. I mean, I could have held out, but after a while I just got to thinking, "Well, why not? Try it and see if you like it." It was more or less a curiosity thing. I never really stopped to think about what I was doing. I never really thought about the consequences. Perhaps if I had, I never would have gone through with it. If only I had understood these things, and the fact that I was a leader to the many people in school who came to me for advice. I dispensed it as if I were a Junior Ms. Ann Landers.

Unfortunately, when it came to making one of the most important decisions in my life I failed. In doing so, I also failed my best friend. She wanted me to be strong so she would not fall – she wanted a reason to say no, but when she fell, she fell hard. During the course of our stormy relationships she became pregnant – twice! Choosing to end both pregnancies through abortion, rather than face life in an unhappy relationship with a man (boy) who had become abusive.

You ask, "Why did she do it? Why didn't she use birth control?" To answer that, I'd have to go back to the reasons we had sex in the first place. When you have no clearly defined value system of your own, it is only a matter of time before you begin to cross all barriers. In order to have a clearly defined value system; you must have enough knowledge of that value system in order to make decisions. The system we had was warped. So it stands to reason that our decisions would be warped as well. And who were adults, but older versions of us in many cases, so how could we talk to them? So what did we do? We made bad decisions that affected us for the rest of our lives.

King Solomon recognized that the erotic passions of youth can be aroused before a relationship of true commitment and true love can be established. In an article, "Waiting Until the Right Time" written for the <u>Life Study Bible</u>, the author asserts that biblical love demands commitment and delights in the gift of sexual pleasure within the committed relationship of marriage. This is a bond in which both parties are growing together and being enriched, emotionally, spiritually and physically. The author continues by saying that sex is a jewel that must await the right setting . . . it is perilous to awaken passion before that setting has been provided. Our lives were proof that jewels in the wrong setting do not look like jewels.

Both my friend and I have been blessed with wonderful husbands and families but we paid a heavy price for our youthful indiscretions. Two beautiful babies were killed as a result of our selfish actions. We both suffered mental and emotional stress from these affairs and carried this excess baggage into every relationship we had afterwards.

Why do I say I killed my best friend's babies? Because I did, as surely as if I had performed the procedure myself. I will not debate the ethics of abortion here, for that is not the purpose of this essay. What matters is that at eighteen years of age, she should never have had to make those decisions in the first place.

Looking back, I know that we were the single most important sphere of influence on each other's lives. We were the most important weapons we had against all the pressure. All it would have taken was for one of us to be strong enough to say no!

Denise Thomas

RIPPLES OF ANGER, I

Is it October, November or is it really December
I don't care
What about my hair
That's not really the subject
It tears me apart to know my heart is
Break
    ing
No, broken it is
Who cares what it is
What words go unspoken
I dare you to say something to me
Can't u see the ripple of anger
No, you don't see past your own throat

You can't see
Blind
Blind
Blind
You can't see me cryin'
You can't see me crying . . .
I just shut up on the inside and outside
RIPPLES of ANGER

Do you know that it's me who is hurting on the
inside of your flock?
You don't, or you won't. . . acknowledge my
pain

I can't tell
Oh well
RIPPLES of ANGER
The hurt the pain
What have I to gain from this inside of me?
It hurts . . . hurts so much I can't stand it
Control
Control
Can I be bold to say
What is really on my mind?
Behold
Behold
I am told,
Just sit back, hold your tongue.
Is that right?
Should I not take flight
With the plight that drives me or sit back and try
to relax
And think about the pleasures of life
Rehearse
Rehearse
Is it my curse
I must know everything to say
Why not know how to flow
With what is really inside of me?

Teisha Durham

BABE'S HEART STILL BLEEDS

My heart still bleeds Dear Lord
I'm crying and I don't know what to do . . .
Even though I know what's right
I sin, then I come right back to you
You know my pain, my struggles and all
feelings I go through
Yet . . . when I mess up my convicted heart
turns back to you
Father God, you've always held my hand and
never led me astray
But how do I forget those times when the devil
had his day?

Like the time when I met WB and he smiled so
brightly at me.
I thought he was nice, (too old perhaps), still I
let him come into me mistakenly thinking he
would be my first, my last, my one and only
But the snakes came toiling on the playground
in my mind
I knew it was better to be obedient and let him
go this time

Then came along BW, he seemed like a nice
guy at the time

He was also sweet and nice until I let him in my
mind
Before I knew what happened
We were walking down the aisle
The devil crept right back into my new
relationship
Lord, it started off really rocky,
The foundation crumbled from the start
I later realized that it was because YOU were
not a part
That was quite the experience Father and though
that's over Some lessons I keep on learning
even though I'm older now

Then there was a friend I crushed on for many
years
He listened to my heartache and wiped away
some . . . tears
I let him get too close . . . that's when this
relationship begins
Not just co-workers, we became much more
than friends
It lasted all too short and when he moved away
It didn't hit till some years later that I love him
to this day
How quickly I forgot him when I met this PJ
Grin
It wasn't long, before he and I, would fall right
into sin
Lord I wonder what is wrong with me I strive to
do what's right

Why do I keep allowing men to feed my
appetite?
Or is it really men that influence my thoughts
within?
Could it be that I've allowed the Devil to use me
again?

A lesson was not learned that time and how
quickly I forgot
When I met TDB at a new job that I got
He was handsome,
strong and knew you Lord —
He walked uprighteously
But his walk with You was skewed when he got
involved with me
We tried to just be friends, but there was hurt
we both endured
Our closeness crossed the line . . .
Your voice we never heard
But when we woke up, our hearts were
convicted, because we knew Your Word and
although we went our separate ways I still think
of him to this day
Often times I wonder, "Does he still think of me
when he prays?"
Again that lesson has not been learned even to
this day

In recent years I met another who I will just call
MLK.
He was established, charming, smart and too old
to say the least

We too found solace in one another as we
partook of a fleshly feast
Just like that, the feast was over, as if he never
knew my name
My heart bled for a long time afterward, no
longer up for games
This flesh has become too much for me Lord
and I don't know what to do
Father, please help me get out of this situation,
as only You can do

Lately Lord we've grown closer in my journey
to know you better
Yet my heart still aches . . . even as I write this
letter
Lord please tell me the lesson as I don't have
much more time — the devil is hard at work
planting seeds within my mind
Father, though I'm older now, I still feel empty
inside
Not even sure this journey is worth taking such
a long, long ride
You know what's best for me, Father; still I
stray away from you
In my own attempts to heal the loneliness I have
shared with You
Did I forget to mention AF who I met thru a
mutual friend?
He *too* seemed nice, that's where *this* story
begins
We talked and texted a few times on the
telephone

It was only . . . a week and a half before I let
him in my home
Lord, I fell short again in my attempt of wanting
to be loved

So stupid of me to get with a guy and he not
wear a glove
We barely knew each other and were engaging
in sin
Just as quickly as it started was how quickly it
would end
He hasn't called me back, Lord, and I barely
knew his name.
I can't begin to describe the hurt, the anger, the
fear, the shame...

Lord what is the lesson you have for me?
Because I am tired of this pain
I ask for your healing now in Jesus' name.

Into your hands Father so Babe's heart bleeds
no more . . .

> *Consecrate me Lord and give me the
> strength I need as you take me through
> this process. Please show me and remind
> me how I need to depend on You
> constantly for everything. Father, I don't
> want be involved in anymore dead
> relationships; sever all ties to those men
> in my past.*

Cleanse me Lord. I want a new life.
Make me a better woman and prepare
me to be the right (eous) man's wife.
                Amen.

Judi Gazaway

THE FUNERAL

She mourned —
Not for the deceased,
But for herself
For her loss —
Of dreams,
Of hope,
Of patience,
Of love
Of self

Selener Fields

MY TESTIMONY

I can see the angels discussing me
And I hear the whispers

I feel the tube in my throat
The nurse's hands
And my ex-husbands touch
God is using this to reunite us as friends

I lay here
Unable to turn on my own
I cannot change my own clothes
I cannot eat and I cannot speak

Lord speak to me!
Will I die?
Or am I to stay?
Hearing no voice
Finding no answers
I prepare to die
Knowing that this death is for my good…

September 29, 1942-June 21, 2001

GATHERING THE WISDOM FROM BROKEN WINGS

"Thou wilt say then, the branches were broken off,
that I might be grafted in."
(Romans 11:19)

We often feel the most alone during seasons of brokenness. Even Job who had done all he knew to be pleasing and right in the eyes of an Almighty God, experienced brokenness. Job endured loss of wealth, family, and health, yet he continued to have a need for God and sat yielded for His use. Sometimes when we are experiencing the very best or the very worst in life, we forget that who we are is hid in Christ. He placed purpose on the inside of us and He wants to reveal it to us. Whether through sin, generational curses, or the allowance of God himself, brokenness is necessary in our lives. We are all called to experience "breaking" in our lives.

It is during these times of brokenness that we search for relief — at least an answer for why we are experiencing such loss, pain, and devastation. The woman with the issue of blood sought relief and healing of her issue for twelve years. She went to every sort of doctor and suffered through their "treatment" of her, until she finally came to a place of needing God enough to press her way through the crowd and reach out to the only person she believed had the answer and resolution to her issue: Jesus.

Despite the pain we suffer, God is there through it all, hoping we will allow Him to show us who we are and how much He loves us. It causes us to focus on what is important and who is important. It places a mirror in front of us so we can see ourselves as we currently are, and not who we tried to shape ourselves into for the future. *"For I know the thoughts that I think toward you, saith the LORD, thoughts of peace, not of evil, to give you an expected end."* *(Jeremiah 29:11)*

1. If your wings are broken right now, what have you resolved to do during this season? Are you experiencing loss? Can you define it? Are you yielded to God for Him to use the loss as He pleases? If He chooses not to restore what you lost, will you still love and serve Him?

2. Do you need to solicit the support of others to help you through this season of brokenness? Who are they and what is stopping you from connecting with them? If you don't feel that you have a

support system, how will you maintain your strength?

3. How can you use your experience with broken wings to help someone else make it through what you have, or are currently encountering?

FEAR OF FALLING:
The Season of Nurturing

The pain we feel after being broken makes us afraid. We may find ourselves crying or reaching out for support outside of ourselves. The **Fear of Falling** —fear of breaking our wings again cripples us and we are afraid to move. It takes time to gather our strength, to step off of the ledge of faith, so in the meantime we find a place of rest where we can be nurtured back to health and wholeness.

Nicole Colvin

GATHER ENOUGH FOR THE DAY
(Prayer)

Help me oh Lord, to gather just enough for
today.
Help me do what I am supposed to do
And leave the rest to you.
I want to pass the test you give
And in my life, these lessons continue to live

Calm me oh Lord, let me bask in You today.
Slow down my breathing and heartbeat
So I can hear the words You say.
Help me see the manna You send and
Gather enough just for today.

Amen.

Teri Miller Barker

A CHILD OF OUR OWN

For this child I prayed: and the Lord hath given me my petition which I asked of him.
I Samuel 1:27

As soon as we were married, my husband and I decided that we wanted to have children right away. I wanted a girl. He wanted a boy. We decided on two, and whatever God blessed us with, we'd be satisfied. We had it all figured out. Or so we thought. I quit taking birth control pills and became pregnant. Six weeks into the pregnancy, I started cramping and hemorrhaging, and miscarried. I was hurt and disappointed, but my gynecologist explained that this was not an uncommon occurrence. "You are both young and healthy," she assured me. "Give yourselves time to recover emotionally, and try again in five or six months." So we did. I became pregnant again. I kept all of my doctor's appointments. I took my prenatal vitamins everyday. I exercised. I ate nutritional foods. My first trimester, the most fragile and most critical, was a breeze because I was doing everything by the book.

Once I entered my fourth month, I let down my guard. I felt like I'd passed the delicate stage in my pregnancy. Just as I was starting to relax and feel secure, I started feeling crampy. I called my doctor, explained my symptoms, and was told to come in right away. Shortly after I arrived at the doctor's office, I miscarried. I'd just experienced a second miscarriage, and no one could give me any answers that I could find acceptable. Their answers were too vague and senseless to me.

I've always been an avid reader, so I started reading and researching all the literature that I could get my hands on that talked about how to cope with the loss of an unborn child. I noticed in my reading that the authors would always suggest that the grieving mom direct her focus to something positive that would occupy her mind. Something that would be fulfilling, rewarding and that would give her a sense of accomplishment. I enrolled in classes at Sinclair Community College which were just the diversion I needed to help me relax and redirect my focus. I read stories in the Bible that dealt with barren women like Sarah and her husband Abraham who had to pray for a child. Sarah was in her nineties when she was blessed with Isaac. Isaac prayed for his wife, Rebekah, to conceive and she bore twins, Esau and Jacob. Manoah's wife was barren; she prayed for a child and was blessed with Samson.

Hannah's husband prayed for her to conceive, and she bore Samuel. Elizabeth, who was well stricken in years, conceived John (Jesus' cousin) after her husband prayed for her. The Bible was full of inspirational and uplifting stories. During this relaxed period, I conceived again. I couldn't allow myself to be excited. In a few weeks, I miscarried. I wasn't as devastated as with the previous miscarriages, I'd become numb.

Just like I wouldn't allow myself to feel any excitement, I wouldn't allow myself to hurt. Once again, no one had any acceptable or reasonable answers. I was beginning to realize that my dilemma had even the doctors puzzled. It was at this point that I started to question my worthiness to be a mother. I was starting to believe that maybe this was God's way of telling me that I was not cut out for motherhood. But I refused to accept that because the Bible tells us to "be fruitful and multiply."

My doctor referred me to a fertility specialist in Cincinnati, Ohio. Based on our discussion and my medical records, he determined that I was a good candidate for in-vitro fertilization. His passion and enthusiasm for his work made me feel that I could trust my situation to him. I was just as excited as he was until he started quoting the astronomical costs of fertility medicine and the procedure itself. Not to mention, there weren't any guarantees that I would carry the pregnancy to term. And if I did miscarry, we couldn't afford to repeat the procedure. I don't remember what he told me the success rate for In Vitro Fertilization (IVF) was, but I do remember that it was a low percentage. Hurt and discouraged, I called my husband and explained everything the way it had been explained to me. My doubts and fears dissipated when he told me, "Teri, if you pray for it, I'll pay for it." And I agreed. This was our first time joining our faith for a common goal and trusting that our prayers would be answered. We decided that we would do in-vitro as our last attempt to have a child of our own.

During the next few weeks, I received fertility shots daily. I was beginning to feel like a pin cushion – I was getting injections at home everyday, and blood drawn at the doctor's office every few days. They were monitoring how I was responding to the fertility drug and watching my hormone levels. Eventually our eggs and sperm were taken, and fertilization took place in a little, plastic Petri dish.

A few days later, the embryos were inserted into my womb. On prior visits, the IVF doctor was very jovial and laid back, but on this day, he was serious. "All I can do is the IVF portion of the reproduction process, but only God can create a baby," he explained when the procedure was over.

A couple of weeks later, a nurse called with the good news: "Mrs. Barker, you're pregnant," she said with a smile in her voice. She was happy to inform us that the pregnancy test had come back positive; a lot of women don't conceive the first time. We were elated because we knew that God understood our financial situation, and knew that we couldn't afford the several attempts that are sometimes necessary before positive results are obtained. The first five months of my pregnancy were painless and carefree. Then suddenly, without warning, things changed. I started hemorrhaging, and losing massive amounts of blood. I was certain that I'd lost another pregnancy. On the way to the hospital I prayed, "God, I put my situation in your hands, because if I lose another baby, I think I'll lose my mind with it." Before I could finish my prayer, I got a calm, reassuring feeling that everything was going to be all right, that my baby was going to be just fine, and that I needn't worry.

Upon examination, I was told that my condition was called *placenta previa*. As the uterus grows, the placenta is supposed to move upward, but mine wasn't. I was told that I'd have to stay in the hospital until I delivered. The periodic, light bleeding and Braxton Hicks contractions made my pregnancy so touch-and-go that I was monitored around the clock. Around my sixth month, I was beginning to get a feel/ understanding of the baby's personality; strong-willed and determined. She had to be. I'd threatened to lose her a few times, but she kept holding on. I didn't quite make it full term, I delivered in my eighth month. After three devastating miscarriages, we received a precious miracle – a beautiful blessing that we named Teryn.

I am not certain why I had a difficult time conceiving and maintaining pregnancies. I learned that everything happens for a reason — in God's timing, not our own. It wasn't until my difficult journey into conception, childbearing and childbirth, did I realize that babies are nothing short of a miracle. In some cases, babies may be unplanned, or even unwanted, but certainly not an accident. In my pursuit of motherhood, I learned that life is a gift from God, and women are enormously blessed when given the opportunity to have the rewarding, physical, mental, emotional, and spiritual experience of birthing a child.

LETTING GO

I'm just going to back off, my Dear Lord,
And totally put my life in Your hands.
I need to rely on Your Holy Word
And not be influenced by life's demands.
I need to let go and follow Your lead
Because You always know what's right for me.
I have been Your child all my life, indeed.
I was blind, but with faith in You, I see.
I should cast all of my cares upon You
And quit letting things worry me so much.
But letting go is very hard to do
Because I have used worry as my crutch.
Life is too short to worry all the time,
So I'll let things go for peace of mind.

AvalynAbijah

BABYLON BURNING @ HER BACK
Canto I

Every glistening silver & sun-streaked strand
boldly entwined.
Soft organic locks gently framing a caramel
bronzed
heart-shaped face.
Features: mélange Afri-Euro-Carib & Cherokee.
Evidencing faded capacity to feign smiles,
delight,
or interest.
Mineral veiled complexion too sheer to hide
behind. . .
Babylon is burning @ her back.
Yearning to look, to glance longingly @ once
before
inviting scenes & dwelling places,
cloaked in counterfeit opportunities and
deceptivity in most cases.
She remembers Lot's wife. . .

Reluctance, her friendly enemy ever willing to
play, distract & divert. . .
begs to tag along – a taunting diva . . . ever
ready to besmirch the divinely natural flow,
with fluff & outright lies. . .

Using her best to flatter & dissuade, to derail
destiny, steal longevity, and snatch divine
receptivity. . .

But the dreams come now both night & @ day
visions. . .
Increasingly vivid, ethereal, dreams w/in
dreams. . .
unimaginable digiteched colors, textures &
patterns; threaded
micro-lit beams form exquisite flowing garments
. . .
Arms locked among them--crossing their chests,
hands clasping, reaching out to one another –
circled.
Encircled by . . . humbled by & reverencing His
presence. . .
Their feet holy & beautiful . . . unaffected by
gravity
So no one looks back, no longing glances
@ Babylon burning . . . @ their backs . . .

BABYLON BURNING @ HER BACK

Canto II

Weary eyelids blink continuously
over wide glistening almond shaped eyes.
Hot kaleidoscope tears welling, spilling . . .
every existing color a prism reflected in her –
issues long deflected. . .
Endless Speculations, Unknown Generations,
Longing Imaginations
Dire Realizations, Missed invitations. . .
Illusion doors slam shut.
Faith . . . the substance unseen becomes most
real.
Her spirit-self – made in His image emerges
Boldly before her, beautifully & unprecedented.
. .
All consuming . . . material longings of old now
aflame in Holy Ghost fire.
Hot tears flow, life-things crystallized within
each one
rolling beyond black-velvet fringed eyelashes.
Divine healing taking place. . .
Becoming Spirit-filled with El-Elyon's divinely
perfected love.
Heart's reservoir of memoirs cleansed by His
omnipotent & precious blood.
Mind: Christ-Like.

Self-will: no longer competes – lined up with
His.
Pre-determined destiny now unfolding in its set
time. . .
Broken . . . Accepting His Will. . . Light
shining.
My Treasure: All HIS.
HIS Will: All Mine. . .

Tanika M. Carwile

TESTIMONY ON OBEDIENCE

For two years, the Lord dealt with me in regards to leaving the church I had been a member of all of my life. I knew in my heart that it was time . . . but because this is where I was born, raised, saved, etc., I knew that I shouldn't leave. I thought that if I continued to work in the youth ministry that God would get the glory. I began to communicate to a friend who prayed with me and gave me words of wisdom after we attended a Women's Retreat. Ironically the theme was: "What's Inside of Me?" The Lord consistently revealed Himself to me and I continued to be disobedient.

In April 2007 I had a disagreement with my former Pastor and his wife. After a meeting, I informed him that I would take a leave of absence from the church. God spoke to me, "You should have done what I told you to do a long time ago." I began to pray, fast, and lay before Him to seek His guidance. The last week in July, the Lord woke me up and told me, "Today is the day that you will resign. Write your letter." I was obedient.

Because of my obedience I saw God move in many ways. Within four months my life was changed. On the first Sunday in August, I attended and joined Soul Harvest Church and Ministries. I moved into my own apartment and was promoted financially on my job. All I could say was "WOW!!!" What I want you to learn from my testimony is that when you are in line with God's plan, He does everything in order and on time. Spiritually, Physically. Financially.

Be obedient!

Sylvia Jewett
(Age 67)

APPRECIATE WHAT YOU GOT

If you love him or her let them <u>know,</u>
If you're not sure of your feelings let them <u>go.</u>

If your heart beats fast when you see her or <u>him,</u>
You will definitely know it's not a <u>whim.</u>

Your body will flinch and your knees will
<u>knock,</u>
You can't stop it with the total strength you <u>got.</u>

Maybe you'll know it and maybe you <u>won't,</u>
Try looking the other way; I bet you <u>don't!</u>

When you go to bed at night knowing you can't
<u>sleep,</u>
Always talk to God instead of counting <u>sheep</u>

Say a prayer; get down on your knees,
Always say "Thank You," if you <u>please</u>.

God will see you through every joy and <u>pain,</u>
With HIM only will you <u>gain</u>.

Let God solve your problems, just give it to <u>him,</u>
He will help you through every <u>whim.</u>

Everybody makes mistakes; it's a part of <u>life,</u>
You can gain knowledge and sometimes <u>strife.</u>

Some of your problems may seem so <u>bleak,</u>
Be happy and proud, above all, don't be <u>weak.</u>

I lived a broken heart ask me is it over? No not <u>now!</u>
But in the end, I will take a <u>bow.</u>

True love will always see you through in <u>time,</u>
Wait on the Lord and bells will <u>chime.</u>

What's for you, is for <u>you,</u>
In time you will know it, so don't be <u>blue.</u>

Don't sweat it, forget it, and watch love <u>grow!</u>
If it's for you, you will definitely <u>know.</u>

The moon will be bright, full and <u>fine</u>
Believe me in time, the sun will <u>shine.</u>

Revenge is sweet, so don't try to get <u>even</u>
It will make you less strong and yes even <u>weaken.</u>

Hold your head up high, never look <u>down</u>
Wear a smile, never a <u>frown</u>

Never kick a person when he's <u>down</u>!

Nancy Sinatra said "Boots were made for walking and that's what I'm going to <u>do,</u> but one of these days, these boots are going to walk all over <u>you</u>!"

But remember "Vengeance is mine" says the Lord, and
"Peace be with you."

Maya D. Green

A PRAYER OF PETITION (HIS FACE)

I'm sitting in a new position,
I look down, see where I was and I
See those who I left behind,
I want to get them to where I am but I can't. . .
I don't know how —
Then I take a second look at where I am
I don't know what to do next.

I look up and see another level that is higher. . .
I know what I need to do to get there
But I'm holding back.
I'm stuck at this level where I can see below and
above
But. . .but, I'm so caught up!

Do I reach below and grab someone's hand?
Whose hand first?
What if my hand isn't strong enough?
I don't want to slip and fall back to that place
So I hesitate. . .
I see the level above and I want to be there —
Closer to Him.

I want to see His face. . .
I want to know what He knows
I want to see His face, I want to see His face. . .
But I'm in the middle
I look below
I want them to see what I see. . .to want to see
His face too
I want them to feel what I feel.
So much in my head
I don't know what to do first
I'm caught up . . . so I sit and do nothing
I'm so caught up
I look above and hear many voices,
Some from below and some from above
I try to distinguish one from another but get
confused.
I return to myself and I know I should turn to
Him.

Sometimes I turn to Him, at least I think I do
I give the answer but I hesitate and wonder
What if I'm too radical?
What if they don't want to hear me because I
was once where they were?
What if. . .

I'm in the middle and I see what is above me
I feel like I can get there if I eliminate
everything below me. . .forget those below and
march straight ahead.
I could see His face if I could just go it alone.

I'm told I can't leave them below, there is a
Great Commission to fulfill
But I want to see His face.

I want to see His face,
I want to be with Him but I can't. . .
I can't because I hesitate
I can't because I know they are below
I can't because I turn to myself.

I want to see His face; I want to see His. . .

Marilyn Joy Pitts Horton

SILENT TEARS OF HOPE & JOY

3 Women. 2 parents & 1 bride. 2 sisters, women now.

3 women are learning to live and grow beyond life's challenges.

These 3 lives are intertwined as mother, sisters and friends.

Each journey seeks divine guidance.

Each has been surrounded with extended family who has shared insight for us to build our skills.

Know the difference of pampering yourselves within your means and over your means.

Life changes because uncontrollable things happen. You move on by choosing how to meet those challenges in a way that makes you proud of what you are doing.

Everyone cannot agree with you that is what makes you different.

If you wear something that doesn't feel good, take it off. Look at life in that way to determine and eliminate stress. Strive to change what is not working.

Compromise is a thought process within the union of 2 minds and the experience of seeing the difference in physical actions.
I am proud of two women I see growing with your life experiences who are not lost in their mistakes.
All parents want their children to have better opportunities; you have both educated yourselves and are further along than I at your age. One with a Master's and another achieved her B.A —
I had an Associates Degree.

I was not able to raise you to have everything you wanted but I did try very hard to provide what you needed.
I smile as I look at you — determined young women of God.

Remind yourself everyday of your blessings and give thanks for those blessings not yet seen.

Understand what you are really praying for!

Don't forget me when I am old and gray.
My heart follows you as you travel the road of life, learning and teaching others what you have learned.

I have tears of hope and joy; yet I know as women of faith you will be successful with your endeavors.
Let no man of flesh take away your independence, laughter or drive to be yourself.

I am committed to finding time and space to seek peace within, which is what powerful women do.

Love,

Mom

Robin Taylor

A PRECIOUS GIFT

Since I was eleven years old I knew my sister would need a kidney donor. When I first knew of the circumstance, I was too young to help her, the second time I was pregnant and could not help. In my heart I wanted to be the chosen one; I wanted her to receive one of my kidneys because I wanted to keep my sister on this earth as long as possible.

Through the years my sister has had two cadaver kidney transplants. The first one lasting only two weeks, the other fourteen years as of August 2003. My sister had to have emergency surgery in January 2004 because the second kidney had failed; it was still inside of her and to her dismay caused her to become extremely ill. I was scared because I did not want to lose my sister; she became so ill that it nearly cost her, her life.

Even though Shirelle was on the National Kidney Transplant list everyone knew that she would need to receive a healthy, living kidney that was compatible to hers. My two other sisters and I stepped up to the plate to see if one of us was a match for her. I wanted to save my sister's life. It is something I can't explain — I felt it would have been stingy for me to sit back knowing that someone I loved needed an organ donation in order to stay alive.

We initially started with Cleveland Clinic. We had blood tissue typing tests, gave blood and urine samples to see if any of us would be a good candidate. Cleveland Clinic felt that it was too risky for any of us because Shirelle had had two previous kidneys and bore two children. They did not want to take the chance that her body would reject the kidney transplant.

My sister researched Johns Hopkins University Hospital in Baltimore, Maryland where they specialize in kidney transplants. I thought the scenario would probably be the same as Cleveland, but after several months of waiting, I received a confidentiality call from Johns Hopkins compatibility kidney coordinator that I was the best match. Praise God! They told me I would have to come to the hospital for extensive testing and to be evaluated by the psychologist to see if mentally and physically I could handle the cost.

My brother-in-law, my sister and I flew from Dayton, Ohio to Baltimore, Maryland to stay for several days. We were tested and taken through preparations for the transplant which was scheduled for March 20, 2005. I trusted God and I did not expect anything to go wrong. I took the necessary provisions to ensure that my daughter was cared for during the transition and afterward until I was stable. The healing process was not easy for me. Shirelle who had always been sick, was healthy after the transplant. I had to rebuild as if I were a newborn by learning how to breathe and complete other simple tasks.

I remember many people came from all over to show support. They thanked me, hugged me and told me things like, "God will bless you abundantly." They commented that I was doing a monumental thing. People were overwhelmed with the idea of me doing such a tremendous thing for my sister. I give God all the glory. I wanted to show a blessing to my sister and allow God to use me and move through me for her sake.

Before the surgery, I felt like a lost soul. My life was unstable in relationships, employment and within my family. I wore a mask to try to fit in everywhere I went, but I was living in a hole of depression. When I recovered from the surgery, not only did I realize that God had chosen me to help save my sister's life but my eyes were opened to the possibilities that I could be more, and do more with my life. I finally felt that my life had meaning. My family seemed to be disappointed in me and my poor choices before, but in their eyes I became visible again. Giving Shirelle my kidney gave us both a second chance at life.

Sierra Leone

FREUDIAN SLIP

I have decided that there is nothing left to give.

I have nurtured
one mind to many
and prayed
for what does not matter
for the last time.

DEDICATION …
is the diagnosis
never to be normal
again…

"so critical I look over the obvious"

Fully developed
third opinion….. fatal
if it hurts expose it
pain is temporary
but the affects are eternal.
Sickness stemming
from giving until the giving turns into taking
taking until the taking turns into regret.

My whispers turn into lies
lies turns into truth

truth turns into the part
of the story
no one wants to hear
 I don't want to write
about pain...
but it is universal
and it nags at me
at me it nags…

because
I am the daughter of
nature…

 and her ambivalent ways
mirrors my mentality.

Climate changes everything
after winter must come spring
there is a thin line between devotion…

self-duplicity

……..burdens of tomorrow
release me.

I am the….
offspring of earned
immortality
on borrowed time.

Reflecting on sunken yesterdays
riding on rolling streams

Drifting slowing……. into
 memories of I…….

Theresa Burrage

STEPDAD

You made me feel loved
You held me and told me I was pretty
I felt safe with you
Knew you'd never try to harm me
You made me laugh
I would giggle til my tummy ached
You did that
You
You stood in the gap
Stood in his place
You took the position without any promises
You took on the task of loving me
What can I give you?
What can I say to this?
Thank you
They call you a stepdad because you stepped up
to the plate
Stepped right in
You made a soft place for me to lie
Where r u now?
Because of u I know what love is
I will never forget you though you're not around
I'll never forget
I'll always know a father's love

Diane I. Daniels

PLEASURES OF LIFE

I always thought I didn't have a testimony until 2004. To me a testimony came from older people who stood in church every Sunday and told how God brought them through a sickness, restored their marriage, and kept their children out of harm's way or a major miraculous situation. Their story always began by saying, "Giving Honor to God . . ."

For forty-nine years I always knew that God had kept and blessed me. Being consecrated with a positive spirit and outlook on life I never viewed situations, no matter how bad . . . to the extent others thought. It all seemed like it was a part of life. Events as an adolescent such as the illnesses of my mother, the deaths of my grandparents as a teenager, and as I got older the struggles of every day living. Losing my job or the ending of a major contract never seemed to phase me in a negative manner. But now, being on earth for more than a half century, I view life's occurrences differently. As my Grandmother always said, "If you live long enough life will happen."

෨

A calm person by nature, I've always been very serious, taking things to heart and understanding words literally. As a result my belief is that because God knows and sees all, He will always give me the power to handle everything He puts before me. But in 2003 He seemed to test my strength and beliefs.

Friendship is very dear to me, even at my age the true friends that I have other than family and my spouse can be counted on one hand. So my commitment to them is a treasure indeed. Of course you meet a lot of people throughout your life, but God has a purpose for everyone that He puts before you.

God's test of my faith began on a beautiful September afternoon while attending a football game about 75 miles away from home. My phone was on vibrate so I didn't realize I had missed several phone calls, (eight or nine) until late in the afternoon. Upon listening to the frantic messages my heart skipped several beats. "Diane, Lane needs you to take her to the hospital," was the first message. "Lane has been admitted to the hospital," was another. "Diane we need you here right away," was the last. Not knowing what to think I called her husband several times unable to reach him. Thoughts began to race through my mind. What could it be? Is she sick, was she in an accident, did something happen to one of her grandchildren, what could it be?

Not wanting to spoil the game for my husband or our friends, I sat in turmoil through a long third and fourth quarter franticly imagining what could be wrong.

Finally I received a return call from Lane's husband. I learned that she had been rushed to the hospital by ambulance in the nick of time to have her life saved. The doctors however, were unsure of what the aliment was. Nevertheless she was asking for me. Arriving at the hospital hours later to find a relieved husband and family members I learned my friend had had a brain aneurysm and was lucky to be alive. When she was able to talk, Lane explained to me that she had experienced extreme pains in her head and instructed her husband to call me to take her to the hospital. Unable to reach me they called an ambulance which transported her to a medical facility that could not help her so she was transported to another facility 10 miles away. Once the aneurysm was diagnosed and taken care of, several others were found. This meant a longer hospital stay and several medical procedures.

Being the sincere friend that I am, there was no way I wasn't going to be there for her, especially after not being available to take her to the hospital, which was probably a blessing. As a result I worked at least 10 hours a day to assure my business was running smoothly, while making sure my family was being taken care of also. I spent many hours at the hospital daily. There were a couple days that I was at the hospital at 6:00 in morning and did not leave until the next day. This went on for over a week until she was released. With Lane's husband not being in the best of health, I found that being a friend (a good Christian) meant being there for a recovery that took months and several life changing situations.

ଔ

Knowing that death is something we all experience, whether it be a family member, friend or our self, it is a life changing occurrence and something you are not ready for. The experience not only provided me wisdom in taking care of her, but brought on emotions through a breakup with her husband and his death early in 2004. Throughout the first four months of that year Lane's husband, my long time friend's sister and my husband's sister all passed. Only God knew at that time what He was doing to me and how much more I could bear.

Thinking that I could handle everything on my own, I continued to live my life as if everything was normal. I was there for my in-laws and friends who had lost their loved ones, worked my business eight to 10 hours a day, took care of my family and did what ever I could for others when necessary. Slowly mentally I was breaking down, but I wasn't aware of the changes in my behavior until it seemed that the walls were closing in on me.

Then God stepped in and took me away from everything I was familiar with, my surroundings, family, husband and the city of Pittsburgh. In June He arranged for me to relocate to the Dallas/Fort Worth, Texas area, for what I now know as a "faith, no fear journey." I packed up my husband's 1995 Chevy Blazer with my summer and fall clothes, computer and printer, business supplies and Mary Kay cosmetics. I drove to Cincinnati for a three-day stay and then drove sixteen hours to Fort Worth.

For six months God demonstrated His miraculous powers throughout my life. In an area where I knew only two other people He showed kindness by putting friends in my life who opened their homes and shared their families in ways I would never have thought possible. God and His servants helped and guided me through situations. He provided me with contracts, food, shelter and a lifetime of memories. When stuck and not sure where to turn I went to the park, paired with nature and talked to Him through prayer. I learned to depend on people, something I was not used to doing and to open up to situations, to which I now know were possibilities. Returning home in December to celebrate my 50th birthday I was refreshed with a renewed spirit and a stronger sense of faith.

❈

From 2005 to 2007 God's blessings in my life were continuous as they have been in all our lives, but as a result of my six month "faith no fear journey" in Texas I am more aware of his grace and mercy. At the end of 2006, Cassandra, a friend I met in Dallas suggested that I read a book called The Principles and Power of Vision by Dr. Myles Munroe. It was very powerful at that time in my life and unknown to me that it was going to be very significant in my development and experiences for the year ahead. The book caused me to become aware and more appreciative of God's great creations and pleasures of life.

The year 2007 was transforming for me. In January, while flying to Dallas, my first stop en route to Puerto Rico to celebrate Cassandra's' birthday, I could have danced in the aisle as a celebration and way to thank God for His greatness. The sites of the sky were so beautiful. The whole trip was the same way; the pectoris sights and scenes of the territory of Puerto Rico were magnificent. Eighty degrees for me in January was certainly a treat. January showed me God's beauty, April demonstrated how His consistency can change at any minute. July 2007 will be memorable. It's a time where everything I believed about God was tested. When He let me know that I too will have a testimony, but it was when I depended on Him most. In July God confirmed that He is my mother and father; I am still learning that lesson now.

Many people consider Friday the 13th as a bad luck day. Not one to believe in luck or superstitions I've always dismissed the myth. On Friday, April 13 2007, I was unexpectedly dismissed from a business account that contributed to a major portion of my income. Bruised but not broken, I knew I'd survive because God had sustained me to operate my business for twenty-four years so I knew through His will I would continue on. The good thing was that I was freed up to travel and look for business in other areas.

Once again God led me to Dallas, but this time to secure business opportunities. Planning to be out of town for six weeks, my agenda was taking me not only to Dallas, but to Mississippi to visit my sister and to Alabama to spend time with my nieces. Two weeks into my journey while in Mississippi with my sister we received word that my Mom was very ill and that we should get home as fast as possible. God gave us one another to depend and lean on through a time of uncertainty; we are a strong family. Having two sisters, two brothers, my father and husband we survived on something my Mother had and demonstrated to me throughout my 52 years of life, her strength.

Listening to the expertise of the doctors and depending on God, Mom went through many tests and procedures with the aim to prolong her 72 years of life. But on the Friday afternoon of July 27th when the doctors declared, "There is nothing else we can do, we are going to place her in hospice care," we knew that God was our only hope.

After consciously celebrating my youngest sister's 48th birthday on July 9th, subconsciously celebrating my youngest brother's 39th on July 28th and my oldest brother's 49th birthday on July 31st, Mom peacefully transitioned to a life of eternity on August 1, 2007.

છ

What a transforming year 2007 turned out to be. My life will never be the same, but I am truly thankful for God's grace and mercy. One thing my Mom has always taught me is to celebrate life and to enjoy what God has blessed me with. So as a result, that November I returned to

Mississippi to visit my oldest sister and traveled to Ponca City, Oklahoma to participate in the 70th birthday festivities for my friend Cassandra's' mother. On November 17, 2007, we celebrated my father's 73rd birthday and I became a wise 53 years of age on December 15, 2007.

Every day I thank God for the pleasures of life. As I sit back and think. I thank God for letting Lane survive the experience of brain surgery, for being blessed with a supportive family and good friends and for my mother, the late Edna Williams Daniels.

This is my testimony and I give all honor to God.

LaShonda B. Fuller

HEAR MY CRY O' LORD

Lord, I've responded to Your voice.
I've given this man to You, every bit that I can
see.
I tried to hold on to the small tokens,
Those that brought him near when he was so far
from me.
I've placed them in a box for safekeeping,
Hoping that one day,
Only according to Your will,
That they may be retrieved for keeping
And brought back to life
To endure everlasting joy with no strife.
Lord, let Your will be done in me.
Hear my cry and take notice of my actions.
I've given this man to You,
Every bit of him with no satisfaction.
I tried to own him and keep him to myself.
Lord, I repent for even thinking that he was
mine to have,
When You hadn't even given him to me
But showed me what could be.
Lord, if giving him back to You
Means that I am doing Your will

And it makes You proud of me,
Then take him quick!
Lord, just for the record,
I need Your healing – now I feel sick.

Penda L. James

ON TOP OF THE WORLD

"So how are things on top of the world?"

"That's weird," I thought. I was taken aback by his question for many reasons. I had seen this man before shuffling around the halls with his vacuum and rusty tin bucket. We had never been in speaking distance but he asked me the same question Ms. Bea asks me when she cleans twice a week. He asked me the same question my Grandmother asks me when we have dinner every Sunday after church.

"It's a lot of work to stay here," I curtly responded and stepped into the elevator. It's the same response I give them.

He reached for my duffle bag, "you need some help there?"

"I've got it. Thank you." I pushed my purse back onto my shoulder. It had been a long night and I was not up for chit chatting. "Level G please."

"It's going to be a pretty day today," he hummed pushing the button.

I wasn't really listening to him; my mind was racing toward my presentation. He repeated himself, "It's going to be a nice day today."

"So I heard on the news this morning. Too bad I won't be able to enjoy it. I haven't seen any daylight since I moved in here eight weeks ago." If he keeps talking it's going to be a long ride from the 35th floor to the garage where Esposito will have my car ready.

The old man chuckled, "That's a shame. You too busy for the sunshine?"

"Yeah," I sighed, "unfortunately I have to work to make my living. My printer decided to run out of ink last night and I had to run to three different all night stores to find the right sized refill. I just have a lot to do." I needed coffee. I hadn't had any sleep and it just wasn't the day for small talk.

"It won't be summer too much longer you know." The spray he used on the stainless steel doors had a pleasant scent. There was something familiar about the man, but I couldn't put my finger on it.

"What's in your spray bottle?" I wanted to make a note for Ms. Bea to use that on my stove and refrigerator.

He held it up for me to see, the greenish blue liquid didn't have a name on it. The bottle was raggedy and well worn. "What is the name of it?" I was getting irritated.

"This ain't nothing but good old glass cleaner."

"I like bleach, it has a deeper clean scent, but the lingering aroma of your cleanser is nice." I found Ms. Bea through the newsletter for residents. One caveat of living in this building is that everyone has to give back. Ms. Bea cleans my home and I donate money in her name to the Senior Citizens Center where my grandmother goes every day. I like talking to her even though I'm usually working when she is cleaning.

"What's so important," he interrupted my thoughts, "that you have to carry everything but the kitchen sink in them bags?"

"This bag holds my laptop. This bag is for the gym. I work out every Monday Wednesday and Saturday morning. I leaned to the left so he could see my purse, "This is a Coach, it holds my Blackberry, day planner and make up bag."

"You do that every day . . . carry all that stuff?"

"This is a special occasion," was my sarcastic response. I just told him I only do it three days a week. I know better than to be rude, but he was nosy and I'm not really in the mood for this.

"All peoples have a built in mechanism that makes them do things to destroy themselves. All that weight on your body isn't good for you. You gonna tear up your back carrying all them bags. . .you too pretty for that."

Ahem. "You're not my type. And furthermore, I could have your job for saying something like that. You don't know me like that," I was almost spitting the words I was so angry. "How dare you make a pass at me!"

The old man laughed heartily, he laughed so hard he dropped his rag. When he bent over to pick it up he bumped his head on the door and laughed some more. "Looks like you could use a week to reinvent yourself. Too bad they don't make glass cleaner for hearts."

Taking no notice of his comment, "What is taking this elevator so long? We're only on the 25th floor. We should be at the garage by now."

"Old Bessie running slow — she needs some oil. I'll have to ask somebody to go up there and take care of that. My legs won't let me climb them steps no more."

I could feel his hazel eyes looking at me; they felt like drills piercing my soul. When I looked at the man, everything about him was clean. His silver gray hair was freshly cut. He wore a crisply ironed uniform shirt with a purple and gold embroidered logo: *Barker Towers*. His posture reminds me of daddy. He seems like a nice man, but he had no business talking to me so much. I broke my thoughts, "Why did you name the elevator?"

"This here elevator has been good to us." He rewiped the back mirror, "Excuse me, there's a black smudge behind you, let me get that." I moved closer to the front of the elevator. "You take better care of things when you identify with them."

I looked at my watch, "7:15! Come on Bessie,: I stamped my foot, "I have got to get to work."

He looked startled, "Bessie is my wife's name." He patted the door, "She and this Bessie have a lot in common. Watch yourself now."

I sneered at him, "Forgive me if this sounds rude. What in the world does your wife have in common with an ele-va-tor?"

"Bessie is just as beautiful today as the day we were married forty-five years ago. She works herself to the bone taking care of other people even when nobody ever thanks her." He looked at me like he was talking about me, "Bessie appreciates being at the top because she knows what it feels like to be at the bottom. She's slow sometimes, but all she needs is a little oil to get her moving again."

"What kind of oil does your Bessie use?" I thought I'd humor him for a while.

The old man took a deep breath as he fiddled with his rag and wiped the elevator buttons for the third time. "She likes to smell good so I buy her that fancy perfume she likes; *Tranquility*, have you heard of it?"

"Have I heard of it? That's my favorite fragrance. As a matter of fact, I'm meeting with them today. My marketing firm is making a bid on their campaign to reach a wider audience. I am proposing that they reach out to a more sophisticated crowd. Not everyone can afford to purchase the cologne or appreciate its fine quality. I tried to bore holes into him, "I'm surprised your wife wears it." He wasn't phased by my eyes.

He ignored my remark. "Tranquility? I'm surprised you wear it." Touché.

I looked around the elevator. I had never really paid attention before, but the way he wiped the doors reminded me that I had never seen fingerprints on doors anywhere around the building. That's one thing I loved about this building, it's clean. I love that it has guards, is quiet and has a friendly atmosphere. I don't talk to anybody, but I like that I could fellowship if I wanted to talk. Grandma helped me choose this place, "You're a single lady, you need protection," she had told me, "since you work all those late hours."

The old man looked at me, "I think Bessie has shut down for a while."

Panic. "What do you mean! I have things to do." I started pushing buttons. "Where is the emergency bell? When is the last time this elevator was inspected? How are we going to get out of here?"

"Esposito can see us on the elevator panel, there is a camera. The elevator is inspected every six months because it's an older model. Bessie will get us downstairs; she just needs a little time. "

He calmly answered all my questions.

I pulled out my cell phone to call Esposito. No service. "I must be in hell." I threw my phone to the floor, dropped my bags and slumped in the corner. I know the old man wanted to wipe the smudges, but he left me alone.

"Bessie only did this one other time. When the building was first built I was on my way to your floor to clean the mirrors. Bessie stopped at the top but the doors never opened. I was so afraid that I started crying and kicking the door. I broke my pinkie toe because I kicked so much. I thought I was going to die from suffocation," he chortled, that's when I realized that every now and then you have to reinvent yourself in order to keep growing."

What-does-that-have-to-do-with-me-being-stuck-in-this-elevator-with-you-right-now?" My teeth would not move, I was so angry. "Please stop talking. I need to think. Everything seems to be going wrong today."

"Go with the flow. You can't control everything."

Another one of Grandma's favorite things to tell me. "I know, but I can control the silence if you stop talking to me."

"I never would imagine you being so mean and hateful."

"Why are you so vehement about me today? Should you even be talking to the residents? I mean, don't you have other things to do than make friends with inanimate objects and question me about my life?"

"The residents are my concern."

With my nose turned up I asked, "Why?"

"I care about the people who live in this building. If you didn't know, everyone is selected carefully. The waiting list is very long, but not just anyone can move in here."

"I've never known a maintenance man to care so much. That's interesting." I was trying to push his buttons; I wanted him to stop talking to me. "How long have you worked here?"

"Forty-five years. I've seen this building go through some changes, but what I know is that no one who moves in here moves out the same way."

"Shouldn't you be retired?"

"Young lady, I am retired." I was finally getting to him.

"Oh," I was sympathetic, "your Social Security isn't enough to make the bills?"

"I choose to work. When you work hard to see something come to life, you work at it to keep it living. That's how dreams stay alive." He seemed uncompromising, "Hard work is good, but you have to find the passion in it. When you lose your passion, you lose your joy. That's when you have to consider moving on."

"It's stupid to waste your retirement doing this. Don't you and Bessie want to experience the finer things in life?"

"My Dear, you don't yet understand the finer things in life."

"How do you know? I embrace nothing but the best in clothes, wine, jewelry, cars and investments. I'm working so hard so I can retire early."

"What good is it for you to have fine things but a heart of stone?"

"What?" That hurt, "I'm a good person. I believe in God, usher at my church, give money to charity, serve with my Sorority in the community, mentor an underprivileged girl, spend time with my Grandmother, coach my brother's baseball team, and volunteer with single mothers." Inhale. Exhale. "I don't have a heart of stone."

"Are you trying to convince me or yourself?"

Silence.

"You have it all sweetheart, I'll give you that. But your priorities are wrong. You're gonna shut down like Bessie if you keep carrying on like you are. You live on top of the world in this building with it's view of the Pittsburgh cityscape and the river, but my guess is that it's pretty lonely at the top. You should read Jeremiah 31:3-6."

"Are you some kind of minister? Why do you keep insisting that I need God?" I kept my eyes on him, "I have lived through the season of not enough and I vowed never to go back there again."

"I understand struggle Ms. Whitney, but there has to be a better way. It is a shame that you can't enjoy the sunshine. It's dark when you leave and dark when you come home. Isn't there another option for you?"

Fighting back the tears, "I will not worry about what I will eat, ponder which bill to pay over another, or catch three buses to get to work. I have worked hard to get where I am, I can't afford to lose it. I refuse to go back to being a borrower, I am the head and not the tail. I don't have time for social relationships. And. . ."

He cut me off, "Listen to yourself. You need a day to reinvent yourself. You need time to let God rebuild the places you tried to cover up with all that *stuff*. You do your part, that's all the Lord requires you to do. He can take care of the rest." There were his eyes peering into my soul again.

I picked up my cell phone, "why isn't my phone working!"

"Actually, I think I can call Esposito on this little thing here," he pulled out a transistor radio from the pouch around his waist. "We just got these and I don't really know how to work the darn thing."

"Give me that!" I snatched it from him. "I can't believe you've had me stuck in here for thirty minutes listening to your philosophies and you had a walkie-talkie to get us out the whole time."

"It's only been about seventeen minutes Dear."

"Well it's been seventeen minutes too long." I screamed into the walkie-talkie, "Esposito, come in do you hear me?"

"Repeat please." Esposito's deep Latin accent was comforting, "you're talking too loud."

"Esposito, this is Melita Whitney from suite 3500. I'm stuck in here with an annoying old man. Get me out of here."

"Let me talk to Mr. Barker."

I looked at him, "Is your name Barker?"

"Steven Barker." His name didn't register. He looked at me and intentionally said his name again, "Steven *Barker*."

"Okay Steven Barker, here." I handed him the gadget.

"We've been looking for you for thirty five minutes because we have a surprise for you." I could hear a lady in the background, it sounded a little like Ms. Bea, "Mrs. Barker says your breakfast is cold so now you owe her a date."

"I'm coming Bessie." His eyes sparkled, "I'm coming my love."

"Mr. Barker, how do we get the elevator moving again?"

"All you need to do is push restart on your elevator panel and we'll get moving. Have someone go up and oil Bessie's chain."

"Yes sir. See you soon."

Within seconds the elevator jerked and we were on our way.

"Finally." I arranged my bags in my arms just like I had done this morning. Purse on shoulder, duffle bag on right arm, laptop on left.

As soon as the doors opened Esposito took my duffle bag, "Are you okay Ms. Whitney?"

"Yeah, it's been a long ride and I'm very late for work. A six minute elevator ride took seventeen minutes!"

"I'm sorry about that Ms. Whitney," Esposito apologized, "We'll take care of it."

"It's not your fault Esposito. But do something about the maintenance guy."

Esposito laughed, "Your car is ready." My Volvo S80 was running. The trunk was open, driver's door was open and the air was on. Esposito knows what I like; I love that about this building. I stepped off of the elevator and tipped him a twenty.

"Melita?" My legs froze, "Grandma? " I turned around to see her standing with Esposito. Was she there the whole time?

"You got an important meeting today?" She was hugging me. She taught me to close my eyes when I'm hugged by someone I love.

"Yes Ma'am." I breathed into her sweater. *Tranquility.* I had given her some last Christmas. I had never known her to wear it though.

I opened my eyes. Behind us was a big group of people, mostly Grandma's friends from the Senior Center. I saw Ms. Bea as she was handing a balloon to Mr. Barker. *Happy Anniversary.* Ms. Josephine, Mr. Robinson, Michael from 3200, Esposito and a few others were holding gifts. "Grandma, what are you doing here?"

"I told you on Sunday I was going to a banquet. I even invited you to come; it's in your building. You told me you had a big meeting." She laughed to herself, "Girl you forgets a lot when you have thangs on your mind." She motioned for Ms. Bea and Mr. Barker to come over to where we were standing, "You remember my friends Steven and Bessie from down home Barnesville?"

Gulp. "Ma'am?"

"It's been a long time since you saw them. We rode home with them from Barnesville a couple times before your Grandpa passed."

"Grandma, Grandpa passed when I was in the eighth grade." I tried to remember them, it wasn't registering. Mr. Barker chuckled; he is the happiest man I have ever seen.

"Well," Grandma kept talking, "they been my friends for years. They know all about you. I shares my stories and your gifts when I goes to the Senior Center. Doesn't Bessie clean for you? What you call her, Ms. Bea?"

"I don't like the name Bessie," I stammered, "it sounds like a cow."

Grandma slapped my back, "You so sensitive. I knows she gave you permission to call her that."

"I would never have accepted your offer Ms. Bea, you don't have to clean for me, I'm sorry, I. . ."

"It's okay sweetie. How are things on top of the world?" Ms. Bea's sweet voice was like honey on my pain, she gave me a hug, "Don't look so surprised, I told Elna I would keep an eye on you." Ms. Bea, my housekeeper. Mr. Barker's Bessie? My Grandma's good friend? Now it all makes sense, "I never knew anything about Mr. Barker."

He winked at me, "It's alright sweetie. I hope that you realize how much you really need a break."

My cell phone rang but I couldn't get to it in the back seat. "Grandma, I gotta go, we can talk later okay. I hugged her again, "I love you."

"I love you too Melita, have a good day."

My heart was pounding; something in me wasn't settled. Tears escaped me because of my pride. I wanted to apologize to Steven Barker, but when I went to open the door, the group was gone. "I'll find him later," I spoke to myself. "I gotta get through the day first, and then I am taking a break."

As I drove out of the parking lot, I saw the new billboard advertising the Condos. Everyone was standing underneath taking pictures and laughing. I was surprised when I saw a picture of the old man and my Ms. Bea.

The slogan slapped me:

Barker Towers owned and operated for 45 years
by
Steven and Elizabeth Barker.
Come home and reinvent yourself.

I made another mental note: find my Bible and pay more attention to the important things. I laughed to myself, "In the midst of everything I do, I don't know who I am anymore."

GATHERING THE WISDOM FROM FEAR OF FALLING

"For the thing which I greatly feared is come upon me,
and that which I was afraid of is come unto me.
I was not in safety, neither had I rest,
neither was I quiet, yet trouble came" (Job 3:25-26)

Sometimes people live in fear of what might happen for the better or the worst in their lives, but many people content themselves with living the best life they know how to live. Whether we are fearful prior to the onset of pain, challenges, and obstacles in life, learning to trust and allow ourselves to feel happy again can be frightening.

Thankfully, this fear can be overcome by remembering and believing God's promises. If we do not learn what the promises of God and begin to trust in them, fear will not leave and we will remain in a season of brokenness despite our circumstances looking better. *"For God has not given us the spirit of fear, but of power, of love, and of a sound mind." (I Timothy 1:7)* Believing His Word helps us to begin to trust again as well as tell us who we are and what we have on the inside. It also allows us to stand against (and through) the attacks of the enemy (Satan).

Prior to becoming king, Saul had many great attributes that qualified him in God's eyes, but he could not see beyond being his heritage and his family's shortcomings (I Samuel 9:21). Eventually, his insecurities led Him to misplace his trust (in man) and disobey/mistrust God. By the time he admitted and owned his insecurities, it was too late and a season of brokenness was ushered in.

God has so much for us to do. He knows we can get sidetracked and distracted by situations and circumstances, but much like His experience with Peter out on the water, He enjoys our trust in Him. It will cause us to do and withstand want many would deem impossible (like walk on water)! Our focus must remain on Him, having need of Him, trusting Him with our most precious gift --- our lives. Understand that you have authority over fear. Study and memorize scriptures that deal specifically with fear. Then, address your fears using the Word of God and tell fear it has to leave.) If you are not sure about the root of the fear in your life, ask the Lord to reveal it to you. Whether it is a childhood trauma, a family curse or something birthed out of circumstance, it is important that you understand the cause of your fear so you can address it and take it over with authority.

1. Do you have any fears? If you do not, have you ever had to overcome a fear? How did you do it?

2. Are there any areas in your life that you have not completely surrendered to God? (Career, finances, provision, etc.?) Read *Proverbs 3:5-7* and repent for rebellion/stubbornness/pride, etc. in that particular area of your life. Renounce the sin and ask the Lord to deliver you from any spirits that have gained access as a result of the sin. Then commit to allowing God access in that particular area of your life.

LEARNING TO SOAR:
The Season of Maturity

It's not easy to endure the hurt, but it is necessary to feel the pain. Allow yourself the time to heal, but gather strength so that you can move on to the next season. With determination and perseverance find the strength to move on and to walk on with hope; that is the process of **Learning to Soar**.

TyRhonda Coleman

MY MAMA USED TO SAY...

Pay no attention to them little boys
They talking and yapping, conjuring up noise
Sitting on a corner where dreams used to be
Drinking and smoking away life —
Pretending to be happy

No, get you a real man and carry his name
He'll love and cherish you,
Treat you the same way he'd want to be treated

He'll open your door
Pull out your chair and try to do more
Because you're his woman, his vision, his wife
He'll love you forever...
My mama used to say

Sierra Leone

PREFERENCE (FOR JEAN GRAY)

I lust for happiness
but fine details are blurred
I hurry tomorrow
but never watch the sunset,
worry about preference and opinions
without a true perception of what is.

I am that inner being,
longing to be wanted on my terms,
masking long-term commitment
as a way to hide my power addiction

My inner-guide is screaming
"might never go home"
while thinking of Gil-Scott……

Sippin' on yesterdays nectar
while savoring the after taste for years
holding the essence of what I love hostage
Mental breeches are inevitable

Connection thoughts of situations
that do not define the bottom of my abyss
but controls my inner existence
Heartbroken by ……..No

cutting me off is the worst
Worry be my biggest nemesis
Spinning, seeping,
Coming up for air
when I identify the next experience to stoke my
ego,
today, there is a difference.................

I give praises to the Most High
align myself with the universe
understanding..... growing roots take time
tomorrow is another chance to get it right
although, pain commands attention..................

submitting to the courage of my heart
Deleting all that I can not change
and embrace the gift of this moment

Teri Miller Barker

TO MY DAUGHTER

As I watch you change and grow from day to day,
I see hints of the woman you will one day be.
Soon you'll be grown and doing things your
own way.
I'll gradually loosen my grip so you can fly and
be free.

But, in the meantime, as you grow and learn,
Life's lessons will prepare you for this crazy world.
Your wings are something you have to earn,
Doesn't matter how high you fly, you're still my
little girl.

Having you in my life has been a blessing like
no other.
I can't describe the joy it brings.
I'm happy that God chose me to be your mother,
But He will be the wind beneath your wings.

Soar as high as you can and set your sights on
things above.
Be majestic like the eagle and as peaceful as a dove.
Go ahead my precious Teryn, and reach for the sky,
Your achievements will be endless once you are
free to fly.

Love, Mom

THE MIRROR CALLED MY DAUGHTER

My mother died when I was 22 years old. She died at a time when I was just getting to know her as a woman and not just the person who gave birth to me and raised me. Our conversations were different than they had been when I was a college undergrad. Instead of talks about classes, men, work, and taking care of myself, she shared information about her life. She went to a bachelorette party once and brought home a genital shaped eraser. The origin of my shock did not stem solely from the eraser (although that was pretty earth rattling!) but from the giggling woman on the other end of the phone.

Who was this woman and how come I had never seen her until now? Following many of our conversations, my mind often raced back to understandings of my mother at different ages as I grew up. There was a time when I did not see my mother as a strong person. She would get angry but didn't really tell people how she felt. She would find ways to respond sometimes to let someone know she was not pleased, but for the most part, she seemed to eat whatever people dished out.

I could not understand this woman – quiet-spirited and "servant" to her parents and family. Admittedly, I began taking her kindness for weakness and vowed never to be "that way." Hearing my mother giggle over genital shaped cake and risqué party games, the picture of the timid, quiet woman began to melt away. Over time, as she discussed different situations at home and at work, I began to see an expressive, humorous, and wise woman. I began to see someone I knew I could call "friend."

I felt ashamed for seeing my mother as anything other than strong, courageous, selfless, kind, wise, and loving. January 11, 2008 marked ten years since my mother's death. Now, a wife and mother, I understand there will be times when I will need to use discretion and it may appear to my daughter, Zoë, as timidity (Proverbs 15:1). Differing to her father may look like weakness or even indecisive (Col. 3:18), but I pray when she is old enough that she is able to see what I saw in my mother. Until then, Zoë shows me myself everyday. From my wagging finger of discipline to my phrasing (and wrong phrasing) of words, she is a constant reminder to me to watch over my soul (mind, will, and emotions) because what I do not cast down, she will also take into her soul (Hebrews 13:17). When I see my faults, it makes me sad but it also makes me want to change them to be better for me and for Zoë.

When Zoë hugs me, it reminds me that she learned from me giving her hugs. When she gives out hugs just when Mommy needs them, it lets me know she got the message my hugs sent. Lord willing, I am looking forward to the day when my daughter will begin to see me as a woman and not "just Mom," and I pray she will see the extraordinary woman I was blessed to see in my Mother.

"Many daughters have done virtuously,
but thou excelleth them all. "
Proverbs 31:29

Annie M. Wright Jones

WHAT I KNOW

At this juncture in my life and as I move further into its afternoon, I am absolutely sure and without doubt, that God is in total control of this world. There is absolutely nothing done anywhere in the world on any given day or hour, without His knowledge and allowance.

From time to time I am asked the infamous questions that books have been written to answer — "Why do bad things happen to good people? How can God who is in control of *all* things allow His creation 'made in His own image' whom He loved so much die the death of the cursed (John 3:16), allow us to experience the devastation of pain, confusion and despair?" How are we to trust and believe in this God? Well, the answer to these questions is one and the same, it is that the true and living God gives *all* people the freedom to choose to do good and evil. Whether the evil is perpetrated against us, or if we stand as the perpetrator, God is the only one who can make us do His will, but He loves us enough to let us make mistakes. If after making the mistake we repent, He forgives us and allows us opportunity to get back in line with His Word and enjoy restored fellowship with Him.

If we accept the fact that God gives us choices then we must also understand that it is people, not God who choose to hurt other people. Again, God gives each of us choices. If He forced us to always do good, we would no longer have our freedom, but live under a state of tyrannical submission. Therefore, out of love for us, He continuously constrains Himself so that we can have free will. For those who put their trust in Him, God in Christ Jesus stands ready to turn the bad inflicted upon us by others into that which is good by causing us to grow in our faith and trust in Him, our knowledge and understanding of ourselves and the world at large. He will also punish those who purposed to do us harm. Those times when we choose to be disobedient and become the perpetrators of harm to others, by doing what His Word has told us not to do (sin), He will turn His head and not look upon that sin. He has provided for us even then, by giving us a mediator in Christ Jesus, who covers us with His blood and thereby removes the stain that the sin left upon us. Those who fail to trust and believe in Him have no hope of ever seeing or experiencing their life's situations and circumstances without permanent, painful scarring, malice or strife. Those in Christ are blessed to receive power to overcome their adversities.

In Romans 15:13, Paul wrote,

"Now may the God of hope fill you with all joy and peace in believing that you may abound in hope by the power of the Holy Spirit (Spirit Filled, NKJV) to encourage believers as we go through trials and tribulations."

In this verse, the word "hope" means to have trust, belief and faith. What Paul wants us to understand is that this God of ours is the full embodiment of what hope means and he will fill us, with all joy and peace in addition to the hope.

Finally, I believe that each of us comes to Jesus with baggage; whether it is lying, cheating, fornication, adultery, unforgiveness or gossip, it is by the stripes that Jesus received in His body, at the hands of His enemies that we are healed, saved from sin and cleansed from the stain that came with the sin. I was persuaded to believe this over twenty years ago and at the age of my early afternoon of life, I am able to give it a voice as I see it being lived before my eyes every day. This is what I know!

Shanna Owens

UNTITLED

I look in the mirror and I ask myself
"What does it mean to be me?"
I stare at me
The answer appears
In my eyes
On my face
In my hands
By the curve of my shape
I tell my own story . . .
so only I can answer that.

Kristin Young

TESTIMONY I

I had a conversation with married, courting and single women. The topic was relationships between singles and married people. From a young age I believed when people get married they shouldn't hang out with singles. I never realized the impact this had on me until that day. I was guilty of choosing to back away from friendships simply because of marriage. Unfortunately churches don't always help. Many singles feel like outcasts and the singles ministries are often a bunch of women saying, "Woe is me . . . " or the opposite, "I don't need no man!" God wants us to function together. We all have a purpose and we must remember that a spouse is an addition to the family. We can't consciously or unconsciously feel less than just because we aren't married. I thank God for the married ladies who blessed me when they shared stories of how they were hurt when close friends drifted away once they got married.

Singleness does not make us less important than married people. If anyone has friendships that need to be mended, I pray you have the courage, wisdom and humility to do so.

TESTIMONY II

My life is so off balance that it effects me physically and I'm just learning to make changes. I admit that I have a Superwoman complex. I tended to take Philippians 4:13 WAY out of context. I thought I was proving my loyalty and endurance. I thought I was an example to lazy people. These things may be true; my inability to say "No" led me to constant fatigue, irritability and less patience. The one thing I never realized was that my off balanced life was not pleasing to God! With all of my praying, fasting and renewed mind, I have still been out of order and displeasing to God.

I now see how off I've been. God is not only pleased when we know His Word, but when we *do* His Word. I challenge each of you to do a self check. How much of your time is devoted to prayer? Studying the Word? Work? Family Time? Personal Goals? Sleep? What about "Me Time?"

Balance is the key to a long, healthy and God-pleasing life.

Gwendolyn D. Buchanan

RECONNECTING WITH SPIRIT

After the end of a tumultuous long-term
relationship
I needed answers to questions that I hadn't had
the courage to ask.

Why had I allowed myself to be a doormat?
Was it because I didn't know myself enough,
love myself enough or honor myself enough?

At first, the excruciating pain of the break-up
felt as if he had ripped my heart out of my chest.
I was dying a slow death—fighting to take every
breath . . .
my heart lay lifeless it had no rhythm, no beat. .
. it was NUMB!

The essence of sprit is to create, love,
explore, feel, share—BE!
My pain was so great; I could do none of these,
I was void – EMPTY.

I filled my life with people, things and
circumstances
that did not honor me.

I went searching for a "Mr. Goodbar" to ease
my pain.
I certainly found him, and he was nuttier than a
fruitcake.
We came together with baggage . . . a menagerie
of mismatched designer pieces dressed up on
the outside . . .
real ugly on the inside.

Luckily, I saw the pattern that was about to
repeat itself.
It was a dance I'd danced before so I knew the
steps and baby, I knew it was a dance that I'd sit
out.

I went inward to the dark places of my soul to
find me.
Connecting with Spirit is becoming one with the
Creator, and creating a new truth.
I hide and seek with myself.
I was afraid to face the truth about myself;
I was afraid to be accountable and take
responsibility for what I had created
It was easier to operate in dysfunction— at least
I knew what to expect.

To begin my journey of truth and healing,
I took a vow of celibacy so that I could flush all
remnants of the past from my body, mind and
soul.

It is not easy to deny the flesh.

"I'm in my prime", she told me.
"I need to love and be loved."
Her justification for serving herself was
relentless.
Night after night, she beat me into a state of
frenzy so great, that I was physically and
mentally exhausted each morning.

I began a romance with me in an effort to
discover, love, appreciate and express me.
I learned to deny things that didn't honor me
and avoid people who didn't stimulate me . . .
Slowly, I began to see love, romance and
pleasure in the simplest of things. . .
eating a meal and savoring each morsel;
bathing by candlelight; and flirting with myself
each morning as I brushed my pearly whites.
walking in the rain and splashing in the puddles.
Facing the truth meant that I had to feel
again…to connect to Spirit.

LaFlora Sholar

280.31

In retrospect, She knew the miles were
necessary.
What else could keep her in chastity and virtue
but two hundred eighty, and some?

He speaks of tasting like a rainbow – he favors
her lips.
She could only think of uncurling the hairs on
his incredible chest, one by one in a necessary
way.

Kissing the corners of his mouth,
happy with the thought of him exploring places
yet unseen.
She could never get enough of his long distance
kisses.

This one, she thought out loud, is worth it
So she'll wait considering the imminent meeting
of
lips, limbs, life, love.

She still acknowledges the length,
the width of the miles that keep her from daily
contact.
Miles inconveniently necessary and fair.

"You need to be a friend",
but her thoughts give way to passion.
A peace. A time. A joy.
 She waits.
Ever convinced at seeing him again, in a more
promising way.

"You lost your choice when you spoke of what
you'd do to me, together with me, igniting my
passions, desires
of what's to come. and come. and come again."
Never quite privy to the reason, still she waits
refusing to consider times, or reasons behind
her perception of truth. She drops the baggage.

Past sorrows, old things dissipate in a constant
way,
not denying the process, growth they gave,
using the promise of the future. Forgiving the
past.

Feeling bittersweet pangs of possibilities, she
waits in blurring movement of emotional minds,
waits to welcome new life ending the 280.31.

Finding some things worth the wait.

Danada Beckwith

LATTE & LORNA DOONES®

A few years ago, my life went through several transitions that I could only term as a *hell of a year*. I felt like I'd been hit by a car. It appeared that I had the perfect life, I was a home owner, a minister in the church, my own boss, married and raising children. The truth was: *I was a public success and a private failure*. My perfect life fell apart like dominos. It felt like I was living the movie *Under the Tuscan Sun*. This movie is my metaphor for the seasons of my life. It took the character through her broken-ness, nurturing, maturity, and freedom all in that order.

I didn't hold up well under the pressure. I would call my girlfriends and hit the club. At other times I put on my fuzzy slippers and cuddled under a blanket. Even though I searched the Bible I was murmuring, complaining and groveling in my misery. Nothing worked. Not even when I drank Latte's and ate Lorna Doones, eventually I began to feel like I'd been backed into a corner. I was failing miserably and handling my circumstances. I battled depression and hopelessness, gained weight, and I was on the verge of turning my back on the one I needed most – God.

When your back is against the wall, you have two choices to make: either slide down the wall in tears of defeat, or come out swinging. At first I slid down the wall in tears, almost defeated until, I realized that a change had to take place. Without doing a new thing, you cease to mature. Changing my ways became my rebirth. The process hurt because I had to move past the *spoiled brat syndrome* and accept the fact that the world doesn't owe me anything.

When I didn't get my way, everyone knew about it. I was selfish, self-centered, prideful, unforgiving, bitter, and emotionally broken. I took childhood expectations into adulthood, lived in a fantasy world, accompanied with an extensive amount of wishful thinking and spending. Because I did not know who my father was, I was looking for a father-figure in men. Suffering in silence and suppressing my pain, everyone that meant anything to me took the hits of my anger, depression, and frustration. Desperate for change, I had to assess where I was in my life. That was the worse process — it hurts when you can't get it right and you want to.

ଓ

After going through one emotional roller coaster after another, I sold the devil back his lie and enrolled myself in Truth Academy. The Faculty and Staff are known as *Face Yourself!* Their motto is "to thine own self be true"! The Superintendent is God Himself, Principal is J. Christ and the Asst. Principal is D. Holy Spirit. Thankfully this school cares so much about your passing every test; they will let you keep taking them until you pass. I repeated many tests in the last year.

At this point, the only way I was going to be able to pick up the pieces of my life was to release this into the hands of the true burden bearer. When I looked up the word *broken*, sadness came over me. I wanted to cry but could not. So many meanings pertained to me that my face should have been its representation. I saw words such as: fractured, fragmented, not in working order, improperly functioning, violated, and weakened in spirit. My mouth was dry from being open so long. I knew then, that I had to accept this journey and become a firm believer that whatever season God has me in, if HE led me to it, HE WILL see me through it! I then said a prayer "So here I am Lord; BROKEN before you and going through as I pick up my broken pieces."

&

I've managed to push past the barriers of deceit to be more honest with myself. No way am I out of the woods— is maturity an evolutionary journey. Here are some principles that worked for me:

1. Be real with yourself if you lack wisdom – ask for it!
2. Come to know that maturity is being able to accept change, conflict, setbacks, growing pains, and seasonal shifts without falling apart, cracking under pressure, or giving up. BE TEACHABLE!
3. Have a repentant heart – everyday in prayer acknowledge your faults of the day, and ask the Lord's help for correction.
4. Accept change – it's hard, but necessary to grow.
5. Faith's first assignment is BELIEF!
6. STOP! ACCEPT YOURSELF at whatever phase in life you're in, admit it, and know your season, because if you don't know where you are, you won't know where you're going.

&

Through prayer, determination, and a desire to be free, I know that I'll be free to fly in due season. Walk in your season! Ecclesiastes 3.

uNique

THAT'S WHAT I'LL DO

I love you

That's right
I said it, I love you

And I'd do anything for you
Anything

Anything that is, except...

. . . be ignored by you
see indifference on your face
be played or play myself
be so far down on your list of priorities that I'll
never see the light of day
try to figure out what's on your mind because
you won't tell me
allow you to treat me like I'm a casual
acquaintance
allow you to suggest that my presence, my very
being doesn't matter
being the only one holding up my end of the
relationship

thinking bad about myself because you think
bad about me
Anything except . . .

I'll do anything for you — because I love you

Myra Michele George

NEW BEGINNINGS

I thought I knew what I wanted, so I went for it. I was twenty-seven, going on forty; I was determined to make my long distance boyfriend my husband. In my mind I was getting old. I packed up my belongings and moved to Maryland from Ohio. Full of hope and anxious expectation, I started living with my boyfriend. He was older than me by four years. This made me feel safe and protected.

It started off nicely. He cooked for me a few times a week, shared his family with me and showered me with affection for a whole two months! I held on to those two months for dear life because two years later, as the shoes were dyed and the dress was paid for, I was determined to make my sin right.

There I stood, at the back of the church, shrouded down in white from head to toe. My 5'2" frame diminished to a mass of whiteness. I looked down the aisle to my future husband. He waited for me with a look of hesitancy. Was it the countless nights he left me alone that bothered him? Was it the days that turned to weekends and ran into the work week where he remained absent that bothered him? Was it the unanswered pages (before cell phones) that bothered him? Was it that marriage license that he was supposed to pick up by 4:00 p.m. the day before the wedding; but conveniently forgot that bothered him? Was it the wedding rehearsal he arrived two hours late for that bothered him? Who knows what bothered him. I knew it all bothered me. The doubt loomed over me as I looked at the man I doubted, questioned and did not trust.

In 1995 I married the idea of being married. I marched toward the altar of marriage into a union with an unfaithful partner to be joined by a bisexual priest shrouded in his own cloak of secrecy in the A.M.E. Zion church. When my husband announced to (pregnant) me seven months later, the week before Mother's Day, that he was unhappy and leaving I looked at him with disgust and thought to myself: *"You have to be home to be happy. You have to work to be happy. Most of all, you have to want to be happy because it's not my job to entertain a grown man."*

Suspicion became fact as his family and friends opened up to me and told me stories of his double life and prior marriage dissolved just three days before the wedding. A son deserted by his own father, he made the choice to willingly subject his own seed that was growing in me.

I said goodbye willingly. I could not live with a person I did not know. My ex was not who he presented himself to be and the façade obviously wore him out. I struggled, moved, sought shelter for two years with family and emerged stronger and more blessed.

I reflect upon the many obstacles encountered while I was pregnant. For the first time in my life, I used the Word to guide me through each obstacle. I emerged with a testimony because I passed the test. I know that I passed because He has blessed me beyond measure. My baby will turn twelve soon and my husband of a decade is my best friend and father of our two sons. My career has allowed me to travel, pay off debt, buy three houses, take vacations, build a college fund, save for retirement and help others.

May you find refuge as I did in Isaiah 54:4-8:

"Do not be afraid for you will not suffer shame. Do not fear disgrace; you will not be humiliated. You will forget the shame of your youth and remember no more the reproach of your widowhood. For your Maker is your husband – the Lord Almighty is His name – the Holy One of Israel is your redeemer, he is called the God of all the earth. The Lord will call you back as if you were a wife deserted and distressed in spirit, a wife who married young, only to be rejected says your God. For a brief

*moment I abandoned you, but with deep com-
passion I will bring you back. In a surge of
anger I hid my face from you for a moment, but
with everlasting kindness I will have compassion on you says the Lord your redeemer."*

Lauren Lake

TRUSTING GOD'S DIRECTION. . . WHEN THERE'S NO DIRECTION

It felt as if my skin was being ripped off my body. What was this force? The stretching . . . the pulling. My limbs jerked in every direction. I screamed, but no one could hear me. My ego laid helplessly on the floor. My pride couldn't soothe my tears. I was in a vulnerable place. Every level of comfort had been stripped away. I felt naked. "Why is this happening to me?" I cried out to God, "I didn't sign up for this!" But, I did.

It's not comfortable place when God tests your faith and obedience. It can feel unbearable, at times, to be pulled, stretched and disciplined in such a tedious manner. But without it, you could not fully appreciate the beauty of an intimate relationship with God. I learned this when God broke me consistently through a series of events. I ceased crying over the pain of going through and began to appreciate God's desire to mold me. (*Proverbs 3: 5, 6*)

In February 2007 I was at a crossroad feeling

uncomfortable, unsettled and agitated with life. I had been working in Pittsburgh for a year and a half, but was seeking a new career. After praying for direction a year earlier, I had gone against the odds and started applying only to magazines. But it seemed as if I was going nowhere.

To my surprise, that cold February night, God answered my concerns. He said my current job was going to renew my contract and offer me a position permanently, but I was to decline it. "What?" I questioned. "You do know I have bills, God? It's been a year since I started looking for a new job. What makes you think I'm going to find something in five months?" It didn't make any sense. Why turn down a job when I don't have a new one to replace it? I needed the money and couldn't afford to be unemployed. God continued to tell me that it was not about money and I couldn't risk becoming complacent.

So I obediently accepted God's direction. (*Genesis 7:5*) Since my two-year contract was up for renewal in July, I had plenty of time to scramble for a new job and not worry myself with the agonizing thought of declining my current employer's offer. Little did I know it all would change the next day.

That very next day, I found myself in the office of the most important person at the company. *Coincidently* my manager realized that day, my contract was ending in July and it would be a shame to let me go. "Really God?" I freaked out. "You want me to do this now? You want me to go into my boss' office, turn down the position with a higher pay, knowing I don't have a job lined up, and spend the next couple of months uncomfortable, looking like a fool?" I desperately tried to bargain with God. But in the end, I said no to the position and yes to God's will. I had a peace about it … then I realized my safety net had just been stripped. Now I was forced to lean on God. *(Psalm 37:4)*

What do you do when God tells you to trust Him and take a huge leap in faith? You condition yourself for the jump. I prayed like I never prayed before. I read my Bible as if I was studying for the SAT. I rolled out of my warm, cozy bed to drive 25 minutes, in the snow, to attend church. If God had a Word for me, I was going to get it.

Until that point, I thought I had a good relationship with Jesus Christ. I enjoyed mid-day matinees, long walks in the park, and curling up next to the fireplace with Him while reading the Bible. We were inseparable and went together like collard greens and cornbread. But, I realized He was calling me closer. *(Psalm 23:5)*

It was enough to have co-workers question my decision and look at me as if I was insane, but now God was calling me to share my story with others? That was not my plan. I had intentions to lay low and share the testimony once God brought me out. But I kept finding myself in conversations where someone needed to hear what I was going through. "It's hard enough I have to deal with this alone," I constantly reminded God. "But now you want me to be a spectacle for everyone to watch and see how this situation will turn out? Why are you doing this to me!" God reminded me that in order for Him to get the glory, people needed to see me going through – not knowing how it will turn out, yet trusting Him. (Psalm 23:3)

It was April. July was right around the corner. My boss had made numerous attempts to convince me to stay. I continued to decline. I had, at that point, applied to almost eighty magazines. All of my current friends in Pittsburgh, left for a better life. Time was ticking. Some days I cried; some days I wanted to quit and take the easy road. Most days, I leaned on God.

I knew I was following God's direction. I knew the reason for the rejection letters wasn't because I was not qualified, but that God had a reason for me to stay. And although I had a peace about it, I still found myself questioning at times. Did God really tell me to turn this job down? Why don't I just apply to other jobs? Will it really hurt for me to stay at my current job? How am I going to pay my bills after July?

My main concern was making the wrong decisions and making God look bad. I didn't want to steer anyone away from God on account of my wrong doings. But God reminded me that I wasn't directing the scene, I was following His lead. He knew the plot; it was up to me to act accordingly. *(Mark 4:39)*

I didn't know three simple words, "Peace, be still," could be so powerful. As I looked at my situation and I began to worry, I spoke those words. When I looked at the calendar and my checkbook, I said those words. When I listened to people give me "common sense" advice, I received those words. I was too far along to worry about the winds. *(Jeremiah 17:7,8)*

I had a great deal of peace in June. I wasn't worried. God told me He would make a way and that He had a magazine waiting for me. I was communicating with three other interested magazines. One magazine, located in Chicago, had interviewed me a couple of times and corresponded with me as if I already had the job. I knew God's timing would be perfect.

> *Jesus, once more deeply moved, came to the tomb. It was a cave with a stone laid across the entrance. "Take away the stone," He said. "But, Lord," said Martha, the sister of the dead man, "by this time there is a bad odor, for he has been there four days." Then Jesus said, "Did I not tell*

you that if you believed, you would see the
glory of God?"
(John 11:38-40).

It was the beginning of July and I had gotten back from a trip in Florida. I was excited about the week. The magazine in Chicago was going to call me any day to offer me the job. And it couldn't have come at a better time. I had nine days left on my current job's contract and one paycheck left. My apartment lease was also expiring in a month.

So as I settled in and checked my mail, I saw a familiar letter. I prayed it wasn't what I thought, but my heart had already dropped. It was a rejection letter from the magazine in Chicago saying I was qualified for the position, but I was not compatible.

I collapsed on my bed and began to have the most candid conversation I ever had with God. "Why God!" I screamed. "Why would you do this!" It was over. I was done. It was too late. But He said He had a magazine for me? He had me walk around and tell people I trusted Him. And I believed Him. Now I had to work nine days straight at my job, knowing I didn't have another offer lined up, knowing my co-workers were going to ask me about my future, and knowing my last rejection letter was laying on my kitchen table. And through the agony, torture and continuous crying, I had to force a smile on my face, lift my head and confess to myself and everyone else, "God will still make a way." (*Jeremiah 29:11*)

August came and I continued to look for jobs. I woke up every morning expecting someone to hire me. I had no money, but I had faith. My last drop of pride left when I emailed every friend and asked for money. God had me where I needed to be.

It all hit me in mid August. I looked at my situation around me. I gave up a job out of obedience, although it made me look like a fool. I was down to my last two dollars and had to be out of my apartment in three weeks. I finally told my Dad what I had done. He said he wasn't going to support a stupid decision and that I should give up, come home and find some random job that doesn't match my degree.

So I fell on my face and cried out to God, "Although you stripped me bare and had me endure this trial, I'm still with you. And I will continue to be with you." At that moment, nothing else mattered. It was me and God. *(Psalm 30:5)*

The very next day, my situation started to change for the better. One event led to another and everything that was taken from me was restored. I remained in Pittsburgh and moved into a new apartment. I became the new Director of Communications at my church and took over the magazine. Every bill was paid on time and I accumulated a new group of beautiful and supportive friends. Most importantly, I gained a deeper relationship with God and developed a greater dependency for Him. And that alone was worth more than anything else.

I realized I couldn't go one day without seeking His direction, even if it meant not knowing where His direction would take me.

Lizbeth Figueroa-Marino

SIGH

I breathe, can't feel.
I drown!
I walk without walking… arriving at the
threshold of darkness and uncertainty.
Empty like a tear without feeling, transparent
and phantasmagoric.

The question: is destiny written or do we control
it?
What to do?
What decision to make and what are the
consequences?
I want it all!
I want nothing!
I want fire *and* water!

I scream out of breath at the cold wind from the
North which carries me far, very far away from
my skin, but nothing changes.

My screams drown in a sea of pride, sadness
and disillusion.

Stephanie Davis

PRAYER OR PROZAC?

I walked down the street with morning rush hour traffic zooming by me. Children were running to school. Bus stops were full of people headed downtown to work in tall elite-style buildings. Yet, I was walking aimlessly with a tear-stained face – not wanting to go to school or work but wanting to stay in bed, watch TV, or sleep; those weren't options. I felt alone in every way. No text messages. No phone calls. No traveling partners. With all of my friends leading different lifestyles, I was the odd ball out. I began to shut down.

I reflected on a recent conversation with my aunt. She interrogated me and quickly suggested I see a counselor to get an anti-depressant so I'd feel better. I told her, "I'm not crazy. I don't need it. I don't want medicine." Although I was quite adamant about being drug-free, I pondered what medicine could do for me. Did I really need it? Was it going to help me or was I trying to take the easy way out? Ultimately, why was I so sad? This crying thing as I was walking down the street had to stop. It was becoming too much for me to handle.

I looked at the National Institute of Mental Health (NIMH) website for types of depression. I wanted to diagnose myself. There were many types of depression but I thought I fit the Major Depressive Disorder which is classified as being a combination of symptoms that interfere with a person's ability to work, sleep, study, eat, and enjoy pleasurable activities. But then I thought, maybe it wasn't that bad! I could concentrate when I was home. My bed was never an enemy and my appetite was forever present. However, I hated seeing the many wholesome relationships as I lacked them myself. I wanted to be happy. I wanted to be free. I wanted everything that I was not. Maybe I was envious. I did question if God had me in a season of solitude. What was He doing? My mind rocked back and forth trying to hit the right balloon to release all the answers.

I looked at the other types of depression as stated by NIMH such as Dysthymic Disorder, Psychotic Depression, Postpartum Depression, and Seasonal Affective Disorder. None fit. So, maybe I simply had the blues! I decided to solicit advice from my Christian associates. Most turned their noses up at me, denied my right to express myself and said, "Just pray about it" as if I hadn't prayed before speaking with them. I left feeling more hurt than ever and began to shut down. I learned quickly to respond to the infamous "How are you?" with a quick, "Fine, and you?" My feelings and emotions became too precious for someone to dismiss.

So, what was I supposed to do? Maybe medicine was the way to go. Nothing else seemed to work but what would people think if they knew I was on medicine? Would I be told that I lacked faith? Would people laugh at me and call me crazy? Would they "cast the first stone?" Was I not blessed with being "clothed in my right mind?" I was perplexed and petrified. Maybe I was wrong for not wanting medicine. Maybe it was the right method.

I was torn. I didn't want immediate gratification but I wanted to unleash the misery. I couldn't keep buying tissues! Honestly, I didn't have a General Practitioner to get a sample or a psychiatrist to give me a prescription. As a result, I made the call to see a counselor. It wasn't the hardest phone call I ever had to make, however, it wasn't easy. What if I saw someone from church at the office? What if my counselor went to my church? Here I am participating at church and ministering through music, yet needing a counselor. Did I not believe what I sang? I tell people God is mighty, sovereign, and a healer. Where did my relationship with God fall now? Should I step down from singing? Through the encourage-ment of others, I knew I had to stay because

God was using me through that ministry. If I acted on the way I felt, I would be sitting in the church's prayer urn!

I was not comfortable telling people I saw a counselor; therefore, I lied and said I went to meetings. I didn't want to be judged. The Bible says "judge not, that you be not judged" (Matthew 7:1 RSV). So why do we judge those who see a counselor or those who take Psychotropic or Anti-Depressant drugs? If someone is depressed or has the 'blues', as Christians and a part of the Christian family, we should offer the same support. This support can be in many forms such as providing a time to laugh and have fun, an ear to listen to, a shoulder to cry on, a card, or other things that could lift the spirits of that person. The Bible mentions at least nine times to love your neighbor as yourself. (Leviticus 19:18, Matthew 19:19, Matthew 22.39, Mark 12:31, Mark 12:33, Luke 10:27, Romans 13:9, Galatians 5:14, and James 2:8) I was fortunate enough to find people who were supportive in terms of offering a place where I could laugh and enjoy myself. Even in that environment, the problems were still there.

I recall coming home one night after spending time at a "game night." We played Taboo, which I'm not good at, and Catch Phrase, which I was slightly better at playing. How could I return from a night full of conversation and laughter to a vacant apartment crying myself to sleep! What was wrong with me? I had to get to the root cause of my extreme sadness. It was deeper than what I expected and imagined. Was I going to be another statistic? Was I going to be another American adult who suffered from Major Depressive Disorder? Did I have a chemical imbalance? Did I need Prozac or another type of Anti-Depressant drug? Was my sadness environmental or situational? I began to think, maybe medicine was the way to go as I slowly became annoyed by my emotions.

I guess I'm stubborn. I wouldn't give in to it. I was determined to work through my past and the pain that trailed alongside me. While working, I was introduced to the idea of positive thinking and speaking my "blues" out the door. I must admit, I tried to think and talk positively but with each step I took, something went wrong. I thought that thinking wasn't working because nothing was changing.

I knew things were bad but I had to remind myself constantly that God is a sustainer. Once I acknowledged and accepted both, I began to pray and seek God's guidance and wisdom.

I looked at the situation and embraced the reality of my mental state but knew it wasn't my final destination. I took a holistic approach to becoming mentally healthy which included embracing my mind, body and spirit. I became aware of my body and the warning signals. I didn't leave out my spirituality because I knew without God I would be in an asylum, jail or some other place.

So, I started to accept my situation. I sat and questioned where I was and where I wanted to be. I began to pray and read the Bible more. I stopped sending and receiving numerous text messages. Anything that was consuming my time in abundance I began to minimize to make time for God. I denied medicine as a quick fix, not underrating its uses. But for me, it was not essential. I wanted the feelings to go quickly to the grave of my past but they needed the proper funeral. I chose the longer and more agonizing route but the one that would help me labor through the countless pains in my life. Medicine would be my band-aid to keep me from hitting the scrapes, burns, and cuts of my past. However, the air it needed to heal would not be present.

I couldn't deny my sadness, blues, or depression. I couldn't wallow in it though. As a Christian, I was determined to be victorious. God gave me an assignment and it doesn't consist of being sad. I knew God had more in store for me and I had to pray and ask Him for help and guidance. I didn't let the stigma stunt my healing. Why would I stay sad to keep from being judged? I started to pray and read the Bible again! That's just where I was. Wholeness and living in God's will became my top priority. I began to get honest with myself and God. It wasn't until then that I found a peace that only God could give. That is where my true healing began.

Karasimone Pennybaker

I REALIZE

I realize more with each new day that burden
is lifted through my worship.
The enemy is defeated through my praise.
Strong holds are torn down through my prayer.
Imaginations and thoughts are broken through
the power of the Word.
The more that I do these things the more my
Spirit grows and my flesh dies. Then God has
the freedom to continually manifest His glory in
my life.

So God my prayer is that you keep my eyes
stayed on you. . . no matter what I am going
through in my life, I will constantly praise my
God. My praise is what causes things to look
better. My praise is to the enemy as water was
to the witch in the wizard of Oz.

He's melting ......
He's melting....... and knowing this causes me to
become even more *undignified than this*.

Kenya Arnold

I AM

I AM the wind beneath your feet
that won't allow you to fall
The occasion of song that transforms your
sorrowful mood into joyful blues
It is the breath of my heart that maintains
admiration
The depth of my soul constants you. . .
I AM the manifestation of bittersweet
intertwined like rosemary and clover.

I AM

I AM all you want me to be,
and scarcely what you wish I were.

Can you see me? I am right next to you.
Can you feel me? I am living inside you.
Can you hear me? I am right above you.

I AM the wind beneath your feet
that won't allow you to fall
The occasion of song that turns your sorrowful
mood into joyful blues
It is the breath of my heart that maintains
admiration
The depth of my soul constants you

Truly, I AM.

Joyce Nelson

FOR RUTH

Ten year old Julia heard footsteps on the porch. She quickly turned off the television and ran to turn down the thermostat. It was too late, the house was toasty warm and "he" would know that she had turned up the heat. She meant to just turn it up for a little while because it was so cold in the house. She knew she was not to touch the thermostat or the television and she must have fallen asleep. She ran up the stairs to her secret hiding place. She felt safe covering herself with old clothes sitting immobile on the hard closet floor.

Ruth heard footsteps. They were getting close. Where would she escape this time? She would pretend she was a princess again or maybe a much loved young lady of great wealth. The footsteps were coming closer. She was cold and frightened. The closet door burst open. . It wasn't him, it was Mama. She was safe.

The strength of a ten year old girl-child is her instinct to survive.

At eighteen Ruth woke up with the sounds of the hospital in her ears. She searched her mind trying to remember how she ended up there.

Ruth remembered feelings of loneliness and sadness; she remembered giving up, swallowing pill after pill and finally how she ended up here, awake and alive!

The strength of an eighteen year old child-woman
is her resilience.

A thirty-year old Ruth was joyful, happy in her new home with a new baby and a loving husband. Her exclamation was, "Thank you Lord!" In spite of life's valleys and storms she has arrived at a good place. Ruth was always waiting for the celebration to end. She was always looking over her shoulder – always playing the victim.

The strength of the thirty-year old
woman
is her love.

At sixty, Ruth has found peace. She has experienced highs and lows: illnesses, deaths, births and joy. Through it all, God has been constant in her life. Her strength, comfort in weakness, her friend in celebrations and sharing her joy. Ruth is in pursuit of a deeper relationship with God.

The strength of the aging sixty year old
woman is her faith.

GATHERING THE WISDOM FROM LEARNING TO SOAR

"I will abide in thy tabernacle forever:
I will trust in the covert of thy wings. Selah"
(Psalm 61:4)

"Though you have lain among the pots,
yet shall ye be as the wings of a dove covered
with silver,
and her feathers with yellow gold."
(Psalm 68:13)

The first step in flying is defeating circumstances, ignoring voices of dissent, and the negativity in your mind. Interestingly, the word "lain" in the scripture is translated to mean "to lie down (for rest, sexual connection, decease or any other purpose), while the word "pots" is translated to mean "a double stall for cattle; also a two pronged hook for flaying animals on." Though things happen in our lives through our choices or not, we have all been snared at some point or chosen to lay in mess not meant for us. It is required that we rise above our past hurts and mistakes in order to obtain our freedom.

Letting go but not forgetting is challenging but necessary (Luke, chapter 6, "...forgive and ye shall be forgiven)." Your forgiveness is tied to your being forgiven. Letting go is not forgetting; it is acknowledging what occurred and all that you felt but not allowing it or those feelings to dictate your future. You survived it but you do not need to relive it as penance or as a requirement of it having happened to you. *"There is no fear in love; but perfect love casteth out fear: because fear hath* **torment***. He that feareth is not made perfect in love." (I John 4:18)*

Joseph remembered the abuse and jealousy of his brothers, but when given the opportunity to exploit their change in circumstance and hurt them, he chose to forgive them (Genesis 50). His deliverance from his past hurts was tied into his choosing to release his brothers from the debt of their sin and release himself from the anger and hurt of his past.

Soaring only happens when one knows how to use what was given to them through life experience to grow and help others. Begin the process of soaring by forgiving those who have hurt you and forgiving yourself for situations you created for yourself. God is waiting. What are you waiting for?

1. In what areas of your life are you maturing?

2. Have you forgiven people who have hurt you? What have you done to release the anger or hate you have held in your heart toward them?

3. If you have not forgiven, what does holding unforgiveness cost you? How is it helping you?

FREE TO FLY:
The Season of Freedom

Ah Freedom! There does come a day when physical, mental and spiritual prisons no longer keep us bound. There is a time to leap for joy, shout with happiness, and understand peace. With our hands raised to God in praise, we release the butterflies of new beginnings and walk in the peace of being a new creation. When we finally become **Free to Fly**, we have a responsibility to not only liberate others as they walk through their seasons, but to remember our power as new seasons come and go. This is a call to receive freedom . . .

Christine Arnett

UNTITLED

He pushed me

I pushed myself down

He kicked me

I kicked myself

Why don't they see?

Why can't I see?

Doesn't he love me?

Do I not love myself?

I let go

He lingers on

Is this freedom?

Not yet free from the feeling

They can see

Maybe I can

Didn't he love me?

Didn't I love myself?

I begin to heal

His grip is fading

I learn I'm strong

He was the weak one

I now see clearly

They did all along

He didn't love me

It no longer matters

I now love me

I now love me

Paisha Thomas

BE!

I can rock my dark blue jeans
A pair of flip-flops and a cozy "T"
Or slip on my shiny black hose
My strapped high-heeled shoes and
A pinstriped suit

I can adorn my head with locks
Twisted to perfection in the direction of time
Or pick it out and do naturally mine
A tightly wound fro
Just so you know
That I'm comfortable with the way it grows
from my scalp
And if I choose, I can straighten it out

Whatever I do I'm aware of who I am
I am fearfully and wonderfully made in My
Father's image and
Created to be precisely me
My laugh, my smile, my heart my personality
and
Every curve and the skin in which I'm wrapped
I've tapped into my identity and maturing
therein daily

My smile is a gift from God to you
Blessing you expressing how much I value

Your existence and
The freedom with which I allow you to partake
of
My heart where I liberally allocate space to
those whom
I deem worthy
Is solely a result of me being me
So I decide today to be liberated
I've traded low self-worth for appreciation and
growth
I'm free to walk in destiny and purpose
Reality and focus; notice too, that you can do
you
And we can inhabit this Earth in harmony
You loving you, respecting me, and mutually
we
Can be free to walk in who we be!

Penda L. James

BACK TO BEAUTIFUL

I had been ignoring myself for a long time

I was spreading at the hips from eating too
much

looking in the mirror
beyond myself to faults and misery —
I did not like me.

I did everything to get my attention.
pulling at my hair
hating its design

waving my hands
trying to catch an eye

licking my lips
trying to find the words to say. . .

I grasped at bubbles,
Trying to catch my desires and make them
manifest
they would not move beyond fantasy

But the day that she
looked at me
as I looked at her

we were one in the mirror
and time stood still.

She smiled so sweetly
so intentionally
so slowly
finding nothing wrong with Mommy
loving me as I was
not seeing herself, but seeing me

That day,
that moment, standing with my Amaris Lynne
I remembered that
I am fearfully and wonderfully made,
I am not my mistakes,
Second chances come to those who ask for
forgiveness,
Brokenness does not last always,
Beauty had been there all along.

It became my reality that I could not be used by
God
Until I learned to love me – again.
For my babies and my baby's babies,
I must tell the truth
Stop hiding behind the victim I used to be and
start living freely.

That day I looked in the mirror and saw myself
again and met
The woman I had been hiding from all along.

Theresa Burrage

OUR MOTHERS

A good mother wants her child to have more
than she had
Just a little more joy, peace, less pain —
    making more sense of it all

She tries to shield us from her pain,
    her mistakes,
        her mishaps

A good mother lets us find our own way
My mom is the sweetest of them all
So loving, forgiving, patient
A good mother is ready to listen and advise at
just the right time
Just before the ripeness
        Never too close to the rot
She may not have all the answers, but her
answers are her own, carved out of the triumphs,
    pain,
        and hope that keeps her heart pumping

I love my mother
She is like no other
She is special to me and given from God to
transform me into a better,
    brighter,
        more courageous human being

Jaquan Johnson

SOAR

Soar — rise high, high as the sky. . .
No longer insecure, I've learned, cried and
endured.
My pain becoming quiet, quiet as the wind from
within now comes strength, power and love.
No one but God is my judge. I am as a holy
dove.

With my foot . . . He stomped on the head of the
enemy. The Lord has released me.
My debts are now beneath me.
The slashes He received are war wounds of
triumph and by them, you know His story, He
rides in heavenly glory. His death, burial, and
resurrection are of pure perfection a most
heavenly selection . . .

Proud I am to be free; God's revealed glory
lives in me.
My wings are as an eagle's, with them I am as
steel, and nothing can kill me.
With His rod and staff He protects me, nothing
can come against me.

I am free to soar, without Him it is like a prison
there are no windows, there are no doors.

My eye is on the sparrow, I am pointed as an
arrow directed to the hearts of men. We're free
from sin. He is the reason I walk this earth,
because of him I give great birth. My mission is
to simply accept the best and resist the worst.
He said "the last shall be first."

I am free, free to fly, free to fly. God has
released me and I am free to fly.

Charlene A. Hill-Ellison

A GLIMPSE INTO MY SOUL

As a young girl I wrote a poem about myself entitled "Who Am I?" Having no idea of the significance of my first two lines, I wrote:

Who am I? I am me. I was created for the world to see.
Who am I? I am free because God lives inside of me.

Deep down inside somehow I knew. As a child I did not know that the poem was meant for me as I grew into the woman God had purposed; I became God's woman through many twists and turns. Even though I rebelled and did not see the transformation taking place, somehow I always knew what others thought of me was not as important as what I believed about myself.

At the top of it all was the unbelievable practicality to look into the mirror and not see myself. It was being able to walk past the mirror and not get stuck on the outer shell. I now know that beauty is from the inside out, it flows and saturates the atmosphere when it is filled with the Spirit of God. *"For now we see through a **glass**, darkly; but then face to face: now I know in part; but then shall I know even as also I am known." (I Corinthians 13:12).*

I learned the following lessons through my journey and growth in the Spirit of Christ: Don't give any credit where it is not due. Anything you are or have belongs to God. What a blessing and treasure He is — *"For where your treasure is there will your heart be also" (Matthew 6:21).*

The ability to become free to fly only happens when you are willing to tear down the walls that shelter your heart from the true treasure of life — the walls that entrap you. You have to make a decision to no longer be a prisoner of yourself, be empowered to move beyond yourself and discover you from the inside out; there you will meet Jesus.

Discovering you from the inside out is the examination of your feelings, thoughts, and motives. In other words, what makes you do the things you do? What makes you do them the way you do them? Why do you think the way you think and where do the thoughts come from? What inspires you to be, and do the things you do? What makes you tick? What directs your thoughts? What is really inside your heart?

While you are reflecting you begin to intensely look back, look at thoughts, memories, actions, and images, look within, and become self-aware. You think deeply about your reflections. You discover and begin to understand yourself better. No one changes their history without confrontation and the truth of what they can be. You have to face the truth and decide you will overcome it by the power of God.

As you discover your identity you learn things about your past that contribute to who you are, but you have to accept and deal with your past to get to your future. Trust God to be with you through the process. While you are trying to get free, be someone who has been changed and who can be trusted, that is where you will find your wings. *"But the woman was given the two wings of the great eagle so that she might fly from the serpent into the wilderness, to the place where she is to be nourished for a time, and times, and half a time" (Revelation 12:14).* Jesus will be in your identity as He walks with you into the victory of becoming free.

Open the door to spiritual growth then you can get to the place where you can envision yourself in a better place, a better situation, and a better position in life. You can look in the mirror and love yourself, love what you see, and love your life because you see yourself in His image and know you are going somewhere. You have hope, you have become free, and now you are Free to Fly. *"And you will know the truth and the truth shall set you free" (John 8:32).*

Free to fly
Is a decision and here's why
It is the something on the inside
that shows up on the outside
When Jesus is that something that does abide
It flows like a river and makes you ever so
serene
It's a powerful force, although to the eye unseen
Its one of those things you're unable to measure
But it dwells in your heart like a golden treasure
It's like receiving blessings that you cannot
count
Because they are so numerous they give you
what's necessary to surmount
It causes you to see things not as they are
But to understand them through mercy and
grace no matter the mar
so learn to fly as you become free
And as you fly, you will see
That you're more than you've ever imagined
you'd be

*"In my anguish I cried to the LORD,
and He answered by setting me free (Psalm
118:5)."*

Yolanda McElroy

PHOENIX

Up from the ashes, I shall rise.
My mourning is past, the day is here at last!
. . . And I shall dance, I shall dance, I shall
dance.

UPRISING

Rise up daughter, rise up from the dust
Dry those tears from your weeping eyes
Shake yourself, and rise.

Take hold of my hand, and be lifted up
It's time to take your rightful place
By those who walk by faith.

Know I've come and given you new life
I've sent my Word to comfort you
So on me, just believe.

Rise up daughter, take my strength and rise
Refuse the woes that fill your soul
Know I've made you whole.

Let my joy abide in you
As you cast your cares on me
I love you so, never let me go
I've redeemed you, just believe.

My queen, my bride
My dear beloved
Focus your hope on me.

Orienta Nicole Eison

THE SIGN IN MY SHOP WINDOW!

The sign in my shop window must read:
"Desperate".
Cause all who apply here are less than.
Now hold up, no, I'm not conceited,
But you need to know that I'm also not
defeated.
By the light bright, lily white,
Stringy hair, skinny here and there,
Idea of BEAUTY.

Cause I've got thick lips, wide hips,
Big ole breasts, thighs and "ghetto booty."
But for some reason, brothas don't understand
this overabundance.
"She's just fat and lazy."
"It's just over indulgence".

Yeah, I'd like to lose some weight,
But that don't mean that I have to take her
leftovers, and hand me downs, or your, Creep,
Creep, Creep, Creep.

I've realized that in every other town but the
'Nati,
I get, "Damn baby, what's yo name?"

And, "Beep, Beep, Who Got The Keys To Yo
Jeep?"

So don't be confused, for the moment,
My size matches my strength and my
determination.
So if you gon' step, you better come correct,
Otherwise, you face immediate extermination!
Cause I'm changing the sign in my shop
window:
NO CHURCH! NO JOB! NO SERVICE!!!

I am "the" Black Queen, Mother of the Earth,
and what I deserve is HONESTY and
RESPECT from a Man.
I Said A MAN who does his best!

So, NO.
I won't be drivin' you around all the time!
NO.
I'm big, but I have to settle for what I get!
And, NO.
I don't believe that you're the *Best Thing Yet!*

Cause see, I've changed the sign in my shop
window:
All SCRUBS, HOES and FREELOADIN' ASS
BUMS NEED NOT APPLY!
I am NOT an equal opportunity employer!
So if you already got a woman. . . walk on by!

But if you're ready to work as hard as me,

Share your heart with me.
I'm definitely open for business!!

Cause I've changed the sign in my shop
window, and what it reads is:
BLACK MAN! BLESSED and SINGLE!
SET FREE!
If you're down for the cause . . .
Holla at me.

Marla Holloway

MASQUERADE

I didn't feel good about myself
I was used and abused, torn and scarred
What did I do wrong?
I became one with the mask, the night anger fear
and shame began to reign in my soul.

I was in pain, yet I danced at life's masquerade
As if things had never changed.
Fear put chains on my joy.
Anger took my happiness, and shame hid my
peace.

I moved gracefully and I glided on the dance
floor.
The mask I wore was pink and pretty, a form of
purity.
I wanted back the innocence that had been taken
from me.
I was trying to feel beautiful;
I wanted things to be perfect again.

I was in my own little world
And even though the mask was
Embarrassing, Annoying and Uncomfortable,
I managed to bob my head
And shift across the floor.

I didn't know

I was fearfully and wonderfully made.
God said, "I didn't create you this way —
To hide behind a mask.

My sheep get lost, but they know my voice.
Step into my presence and rest in my grace.
Why do you stand with a mask to cover your
hurt?
I demand you — take that mask off your face!
I promise to care for you and all of your
Sorrows when you lay at my feet."
"Father," I responded, "so much has happened,
I don't know if I can keep going.
Fear, anger and shame seem to haunt me."
My Father said,
"No weapon formed against you shall prosper.
My grace is sufficient and my Spirit reigns.
You will overcome and regain everything
That was stolen before the masquerade."

I'm being healed in His presence.
Oh His essence — His joy I need every day to
succeed.
I always thought I danced alone with this mask,
But I have come to realize that the dance floor
was full.

Now as I grow I can see hope and a whole lot of
change.
My faith with works has killed out the pain.

No sense in covering up anymore —

No more costume balls, no more dance floors.

Mercy, Mercy, Mercy
Has brought me to freedom!
I am new, refreshed and unmarred,
I am torn from the mask, it sits alone.
I am one with the Father
I have walked off the dance floor.
I need to just be me
I gave God my mask and He has set me free.

Alvina D. Smith, Servant

FREE TO FLY

I never really depended on others. I always protected my family and my heart. I only saw what I wanted and needed to guard myself from getting hurt. Those walls of protection became my prison instead of safe guarding me.

If you feel the need to protect yourself perhaps it's because you have not surrendered all to God. Trusting that God knows best prevents you from having to defend or protect yourself, or even take matters into you own hands. . . If you're not willing to yield to the process you'll never grow wings to fly.

God has a unique way of growing us in Him. If you don't place yourself in His care you will never understand how much He loves you and is concerned about you.

The more I placed myself in His presence the hungrier I became. I wanted to know Him more. God took the errors, the hurts and rejections in my life to reveal to me His loving grace, knowing that I don't deserve it. He gave it to me anyway and that is love. I can look back and say "what the devil meant for harm God used for good."

It is a daily decision to walk with God. The more I say yes and yield to His will, the stronger I become in Him. He knows what's best for me, **even when it hurts.** It can be a beautiful thing when you surrender to the ways of God, He never fails, and what He started, He will finish. He that has begun a good work in you will complete it until the coming of Christ Jesus. The question is, are you willing and yielded? Once the caterpillar completes the **whole** process of being cocooned for a season, he develops the strength to press through the cocoon to his freedom. When it is all done the **end** results are **beautiful.**

I am free to fly **because it is His wind beneath my wings.** I am guided by His purpose and design for my life. I thank God for knowing me before I was created in my mother's womb; and for molding His truths into my life.

"for I know the plans I have for you," declares the Lord,
"plans to prosper you and not harm you,
plans to give you hope and a future."
Jeremiah 29:*11*

LaShonda B. Fuller

WHO AM I?

Is this the question you ask?
I am one with goals, beliefs, and standards;
Goals that will be accomplished;
Beliefs that will be represented;
Standards that will be upheld and respected!
I value my soul and cherish the treasures it
reveals to me when I listen closely and follow.
I am one who has a past, present, and a future.
... who continues to learn from the past as the
past presents itself in another passed minute . . .
lives in the present to correct past mistakes . . .
looks forward to the future avoiding past
mistakes
To grow from present corrections.
I am one who enjoys the art of living in a brand
new moment.
The opportunity for many is rare and for some,
don't exist.
Therefore, I am taking advantage of every new
second, minute, hour, day, week, month, year as
long as my future continues to exist, to express
who I am through
what I feel, believe, and think.
If you are one who questions that…not my
problem – because I cherish the treasures my
soul reveals to me.

Change dear one, is what we all do from time to time.
Just because you notice change in me, doesn't mean that the core of who I am has changed; and if it has, as you question who I am beloved, I am allowed to change too, from time to time.
Nothing is ever permanent, not even change.
So let go of the past...my past that is and allow me to live in my present, headed towards my future with PEACE.

Tiwanda Alston

A NEW DAY

Today, as I awoke, I reached for my wrist and checked my pulse. I softly guided my hand to my heart...YES! It's still beating. I walk to the window. The wind is teasing the leaves – pushing them back and forth and up and down. It doesn't look like they mind though. I see the birds, afar off. Their song is beautiful this morning, just like every other morning that they sing to me, it's amazing and mesmerizing. I awake to their sweet melody as they let me know morning has come and life is still in me. And it is – LIFE, still in me.

Thank you God for another day. A new day. Another chance. A greater opportunity. Today, I can hug my children – all four of them. I can call my parents and say hello. I can think of my siblings and send out well wishes. I can see family and friends. I can feel the beauty of nature. I can taste the goodness of life. Today I can because yesterday He held me close and wouldn't let me go.

I made an appointment with death yesterday. The past few years, death has been on my mind. Perhaps somebody stronger then I could handle the life I've lived, but I didn't have the fight in me to constantly go from one hellish situation to the next. I wasn't strong enough to go on in this tug of war.

I had played with the idea of death before by trying to figure out the easiest way to go. I wondered what would happen if my attempt failed. Nevertheless, I had made up my mind not to struggle any longer. I was not putting up with another heartache, let down or failure.

I was so consumed with eliminating the earthly pain that I never weighed the cost of eternity. I grew up learning about heaven and hell but to me, hell was the life I lived daily. I paused to think of my parents, siblings and children. I came to the conclusion that I was not needed, nor would I be missed. "Lives won't be turned upside down if I'm gone," I reasoned, "this misery and chaos that I live end along with my life."

I was going to make every person who ever wronged me pay. The price was my life. I was ready. I made a decision and I made peace with it. But for some reason, God decided that He would have the last say in the matter. When I went to carry out my plan, the gun wasn't there, but the bullets were in their place. I took one out and shoved it into my mouth. I frantically searched for the gun as I twirled the bullet around my mouth and tried to chomp on it with my teeth. I was angry that I couldn't find that gun! I was angry that I had made peace with death. Although I knew it wanted me, it didn't take me. I was so angry that I took that bullet out of my mouth and laid down to think of another plan to die. But I woke up to find a new day. I kept waking up to find new days.

One day, I decided that if death was not going to take me, I might as well let God take me. And He did. He took me and held me tightly and sincerely in His arms. He held me so close to Him. He loved me. He cherished me. He gave me hope and peace. He gave me joy. He gave me a respect for life. He gave me strength. He gave me a way out and to this day, He keeps holding me. He keeps giving to me. He keeps on giving me life, His hand to hold and His love to feel.

Come to Me, all you who labor and are heavy laden, and I will give you rest. Take My yoke upon you and learn from Me, for I am gentle and lowly in heart, and you will find rest for your souls. For My yoke is easy and My burden is light.
Matthew 11:28-30

A SHOULDER TO LEAN ON

If I hold on too tight ease my grip
But please don't let me go
I'm finding strength

To stand
Trust
Grow
Believe
To let my beauty show

I'm not running from the pain and confusion
Bottled up inside
But sometimes it's hard
And I find myself
Choking
Suffocating
Swallowed by silence
Suspended in time

Loneliness sometimes surrounds me
Rage at times overcomes me
And fear often guides me

I need to lean for a while
Let you make me smile
Help me feel worthwhile
Until you can heal my inner child

I'm comforted by you . . .
The fact that you rose and moved on

If I hold on too tight
Ease my grip ever so slowly . . .
You won't leave me stuck
As I try to rise from here . . .

I'm fighting to get out . . .
To accept all truths
To deal with reality
To move . . . forward . . . with you

If I hold on too tight Jesus
Ease my grip, But please don't let me go

Lena Arnold

THE SEASON OF ME

I was born in the spring —
April 5th, 1966 to be exact.
In my Childhood
I had promise, full of hope, happiness and in
harmony with the world around me.
I thought the world was a magical place of
wonder.
All mine to explore
Caterpillars,
Butterflies
Bees
Play in the clay dirt
Shovel sand
Swim
Climb trees
Play
Sing and dance
And dream Cinderella dreams of my prince
Who would whisk me away!
Until the day someone sneered, "You look
like a white girl!"
That was the moment it was pointed out to
me that I was different.
And I began to question my beauty,
Doubt that I was exactly what God intended
me to be.
It didn't matter how many people said,

"You have pretty eyes."
Because it was always followed with,
"How did you get that good hair?"
Somehow though, despite all the fights and
emotional stress that came later as a result
of:
My parents fighting.
My insecurities
My fears
My frailties
My faults
In my teenaged years
I still emerged fairly confident,
though I still carried all the teenage angst
that came with it.
Emotional, moody, and passionate
I cheered with cheerleaders
Played basketball with the basketball
players
Acted with the thespians
Ran with the champions
Argued with the debaters
Sang with the choir
Wrote for the newspaper
And ran for the powerless political offices
If it was to be done I did it
All in an attempt to discover who I was and
then
I began to understand my gifts, even though
I wasn't sure how to use them.
Through it all I was still that caterpillar
waiting for my metamorphosis

I masked it well because I was still
Fearful
Frail
And faulty

In my 20's
Oh how I embraced life
Reveling in my false sense of reality that I
would always:
Be thin
Be beautiful
Be fly
Be fine
Be the envy of all the old women
I fell in love, got my heart broken
And broke my share of hearts in return
along the way.
But all in all, life was good
I partied, I sang, I danced
I lived and I planned
'cause you know I knew EXACTLY
how my life would be
Set my goals and I did everything right!
'Cause you know I knew all there was
to know-Right?
I gave my smart mouth as good as I got
and no one was going to take me out.
I'd made it this far and I wasn't going
down without a fight!
But in spite of all the bravado
I was still a scared kid

Steady on the outside, but skittish and
unsure within.
The doubt caused me to get hurt
multiple times
'cause the little girl in me still wanted to
be liked by everyone.
So I prostituted my gifts
And used them to help others build their
prosperity
Because I didn't believe enough in the
merits of my own dreams.
I buried my talents in the sand, hid them so
I wouldn't threaten anyone.
I convinced myself that doing so was for
God's greater good.
And I broke down!

At 30
I started coming back to myself.
Something clicked inside of me and said,
"Enough of this B.S. you have forgotten
who you are."
So I shucked off all my previous shackles,
be they, emotionally draining

Relationships
Jobs
Religious institutions
And I set sail on a course of re-discovery.
In the process I found my dreams again.
I found ME!

At 40 I said to the world, "Kiss my ass!"
I finally fell in love with
My fair skin
My kinky hair
My large breasts
My big behind
My C-section scars
And I embrace the thickening waistline
that refuses to yield to my 30 minutes of
exercise
and 50 sit-ups a day!
I cut off all my hair and shed all the
previous connections with the me that was
still looking for affirmation from:
My absentee father
The white man's idea of beauty
My boss
My peers
*And anyone or anything still trying to pull
me down!*
I finally understood my Cousin Carolyn's
words.
"Marie, the people who love you always
will,
and the people who don't won't EVER."
I finally accepted me!
All my faults
All my frailties
All my fears
All my failures
Then I decided that it was ME time!

I threw out the window all my desires to
help those who only pretended to want it.
Time wasters! Busters!
Crows trying to keep the eagle from flying!
I figured I have 20,
If I'm really blessed, maybe 30 good years
left
And they belong to me
I dug up my dreams, found my talents, and
dumped them out of the backpack I'd been
hiding them in.
The final season of my life is springtime
again
It's the season of striding confidently into a
room and not caring if anyone sees me
I see me!
God sees me!
And we both think we are just wonderful
It's the season of me!

Lyndell O. Robinson

MY LEGACY

I don't have to be a queen to be a regal being
Nor do I need to state
that I am the descendant of royalty to be great
My life is my own to make or break as I choose

I can learn from my history, but I cannot live in
the past
I can build on the achievements of others or
start from dirt one
But I can claim no one's great or mediocre
works but my own

It's all a process of realizations
No matter what the past, I must live now
No matter what I'm labeled, I have to live for
me –
Set my own standards, structure my own
priorities

I must listen to my heart, mind, soul, and most
importantly, to my Heavenly Father to
accomplish my goals
I can listen to the ideas and wisdom of others
and keep these things in mind but I cannot let
others' thoughts engulf me and kill my
individuality.

I have to be me, let my mind and soul
be free from the negativity of others
Not that I have to be happy all the time or even
optimistic every day; I just have to be led by my
own feelings, thoughts, experiences, and
realizations

The past is a wonderful place to visit
It is a necessary pilgrimage that must be made
But I can by no means live there
I must move forward and live each day a
separate life
I must listen and learn, but also think and teach

My heritage is strong, filled with beauty and
boldness,
Colored by tragedy and triumph but I cannot
rest upon the laurels of my ancestors
For there is much work to be done – much work
to be done

Pay homage to the Motherland, show reverence
for elders
Pay tribute to all ancestors . . . I must do all of
these things
But most importantly, I must be prepared to take
responsibility
For all of my actions and inactions
Because the future generation will look back to
see
What their ancestors accomplished and not

Whether I like it or not, I will be in that number
In that line of ancestry
I want them to hear my story
I want them to see the very root of their family tree
For within them will lie my legacy.

Avalyn*Abijah*

BABYLON BURNING @ HER BACK

Canto III

Crescendos w/missing notes . . . Exotic
excursions planned to perfection
No embarkation. . . Tags hanging from virgin
gowns. . . .
    Beautiful feet shod in God's peace. soles still
                slick
Renewed endings to create, she thought, replete
with passion for living.
Life interrupted. . .
Now restored. Blood washed by Jesus' blood.

Adorned in garments of praise,
God's Kingdom business calls…
Big sunglasses providing public prayer closet.
Hot white-diamond-like tears. . .Continuously
welling up,
rolling down beyond black-velvet fringed
lashes.
Hot white tears rolling & spilling--crystalline
hearses.
Thanks be to God for dreams interrupted -- for
joy unspeakable now
thru resting in HIM.

Grateful tears—strengthening---internally
cleansing.
Tears of joy memorializing
a resurrected, life in HIM.

Babylon has burned. @ her back . .

Mariama Whyte

HOUSEWARMING

Dana Bowman humbly sat on the edge of the window seat without looking outside. She listened to the squeaking of the school bus brakes and children laughing, telling their stories of how they will spend their summer vacations. The school year was almost over. "Just two more weeks," Dana thought.

She was ready to move on. Her mind was made up that there was something greater than the life she had chosen to live for the past eight years. What happened to her that day was beyond anything she could ever comprehend or ever convey simply to anyone, even her mother. She laughed silently, realizing the simplicity and clarity of it all. Yes. Today, she was ready to make her move that she didn't bother to consult anyone about it. Her peace had come and she knew it was time.

As she meditated, the fresh smell of spiced greens, jerk chicken, and sweet cornbread traveling from behind the kitchen door reminded Dana of her Grandma Mae's cooking down in Florida. How Dana managed to make it smell like that was beyond her. She must have fixed everything exactly like Grandma Mae for the food to tickle her nose that way. "It must be one of those days," she thought.

The sudden brightness of the sun caused Dana to lift up her head and gaze out of the window. She smiled, admiring the freedom and spunk of the children walking by. Stephanie Long and Kamilah Barnes from Mrs. Kelli's fourth grade class strolled by, violin cases in hand, making their way home from their after school music rehearsals. Dana listened as the girls effortlessly sang their concertos. From the corner of her eye, Dana could see someone running toward the girls. "That crazy Tommy Jenkins again," Dana thought, as she recognized who it was. Tommy, in his bullishness, ran from behind Stephanie and Kamilah and snuck himself a big smack in the center of Stephanie's behind. Stephanie's sweet serenade turned into anger as she yelped at the top of her lungs, pierced her eyes and with her fast running self, chased big-headed Tommy to the end of the street and fearlessly bopped him upside the head with the edge of her violin case. Tommy, without a sound, headed straight to the ground holding his hands above his left eye. Quickly Dana ran to the front door and opened it slightly to peep the action. She heard the kids arguing.

"Girl, what you do that for! You ain't have to hit me so hard with that thing!" Tommy helplessly yelled from the ground.

Dana giggled, amused that Tommy had no idea what actually hit him. "It's a violin case," Dana wanted to tell him.

"And you ain't have to hit me like that! I told you if you hit me like that again, I was going to knock you out, and I wasn't playing! I hate you Tommy! Why don't you leave me alone?" Stephanie screamed.

Stephanie quickly picked up her case, rearranged her backpack, grabbed Kamilah's hand and scurried across the street. Tommy sat on the corner as shameful and confused as a bully who just got a dose of his own medicine could ever get. Dana watched Tommy sit silently as he watched the girls fade down the street. He slowly rose to his feet and stood at the corner staring in their direction, as if pondering his next move.

"What was he thinking?" Dana thought. Does he want to get back at her and just doesn't have the wit to hit her again? Does he want to apologize to her, but doesn't know how to say he is sorry? Or did he really just want to walk her home from the beginning, but simply didn't know how to ask the proper way? After all, Tommy was known for showing what was on his mind in strange ways.

"He's quiet during classroom lessons, but always the nuisance during free time," Dana recalled Tommy's teacher, Mrs. Johnson say.

Dana stood still, looking at Tommy's distant figure through the crack of her front door and realized that she could not fathom what was roaming through his head or the heads of other little boys his age. But as he stood there in uncertainty, she empathized with him so much that she began to ache for him. She swung open the door, marched to the center of her porch, and yelled down the street to break the silence.

"Hey Tommy!" she screamed loudly, surprised by her own enthusiasm.

Tommy jumped as if waking up from a nightmare and gazed around the corner to see who was calling his name.

"Over here, Tommy!" Dana yelled as she waved her hand.

Tommy finally spotted Dana and waved with apprehension.

"Hi Ms. Bowman," he said shyly.

"You ready for the summer?"

"Yes Ma'am," he responded monotonously.

"Good. Well, you make sure these last two weeks are your best two weeks of the fifth grade, okay?"

Dana could see a grin forming on his chubby face.

"Yes Ma'am."

Dana waved goodbye to Tommy as he got himself together to walk home. "He's going to be fine. And that Stephanie Long is going to be somebody," Dana thought.

Staring at Tommy transform his uneasy stroll to a swagger down the street almost made Dana lose track of time. Suddenly looking at her watch, she wondered what was taking Robert so long to get home. If he didn't come in the next five minutes, her mission might not be accomplished. Anxiety was weighing on her, and she would explode if she did not tell him tonight what happened to her today.

Dana went inside to set the food on the table. She took pride in her newfound love for cooking her Grandma's recipes. Hurrying to the living room, she turned on her favorite Ella Fitzgerald record. Ella had that way of calming Dana's impatience. Even Ella's blues singing made Dana feel good. Robert didn't like Ella too much, which Dana thought was the most ridiculous thing she had ever heard.

As Ella sang, Dana heard Robert pull into the garage. Her heart began to race while her palms started to sweat uncontrollably. Fear began to overtake her. She took in a slow breath when she heard Robert yelling from the family room as he entered from the garage door.

"Sorry I'm late. I was held over at the office with those crazy politicians. When this is all over, I will be able to rest."

Dana didn't respond. She just sat on the living room couch and watched his large shadow move as he took off his trench coat and began to walk upstairs. Ella sounded so sweet. Robert came to the top of the steps and made his way towards Dana silently. She tried suppressing her dizziness with a hint of a smile. Of course he would wear her favorite navy pinstriped suit she'd bought for him on this day. She grinned nervously while her body melted in heat as he approached her. Robert obviously paid not attention to her demeanor as he comfortably sat next to her on the couch and gently squeezed her thigh. Dana was no good.

"All right baby. You got some good smells coming from the kitchen, fresh lemonade on the table, Ella on the stereo, and you haven't had one complaint about me being late. Unusual day?"

"Um . . . yes," Dana replied blandly.

"Tell me about it."

Dana hesitated and remembered that there was no way to start. She didn't know how to begin a conversation that she had been waiting for years to initiate. Maybe if she'd rehearsed her lines a bit, she wouldn't have been so apprehensive. She took in another deep breath as Robert lay his head on her lap and stretched himself across the couch. She stared at the smooth, mocha complexion of his face. She lifted her hands to stroke his head and rub his face as usual, but quickly reminded herself that she couldn't this time. She was on a mission and couldn't dare participate in something like that, which over the years had become one of her favorite pastimes with Robert, besides making love to him. She withdrew her hands, placed them under her thighs, and slowly leaned her head on the back of the couch.

"My day was . . . good. I just witnessed another dispute between Tommy Jenkins and that cute Stephanie Long. To make a long story short, Stephanie didn't appreciate Tommy's sexual advances, and she basically put him in his place."

"Sexual advances? Isn't he only in the fourth or fifth grade?"

"Fifth . . . he hit her on the butt."

"Oh he likes her, that's all. You know how little boys are sometimes," Robert laughed.

"Yeah, I took my class to the zoo today and we really had a nice time. Little Rashawn was my partner. At the end of the day, he gave me one of his school pictures. On the back he wrote '*if you get a free moment call me sometime*'. Had the nerve to have his number too."

Dana grinned as she recollected this sincere expression of kindness from Rashawn, one of her favorite students of this year's second grade class. But when Robert laughed himself so hard that he almost choked, Dana became bothered. This was definitely not the mood she wanted to create.

"Those kids are going to miss you next year when we go on our trip. They love you, Baby."

Robert smiled as he reached under Dana's thighs, grabbed her hands and cradled his face into her palms to partake of his daily therapy. She tensely stroked his thick hair and sat quietly. She closed his eyes and hummed silently to the voice of Ella. Maybe he couldn't help but like Ella a little bit.

"Can I fix your plate soon," he questioned.

"Sure," she complied.

Dana wasn't ready to eat yet. She wasn't sure if she was ready to digest any of this. Stroking him every day to alleviate his stress was a ritual that she took pleasure in too. Robert always made sure she knew how much he appreciated her. Fixing her dinner plate, massaging her feet or telling her about his crazy childhood would be reward enough for Dana. She loved him for all he did to satisfy her. But today, it didn't seem like enough.

"Robert," Dana was confident.

"Yes."

"How about we hold from traveling to Europe next year?

"What?"

"I don't know if it is a good idea."

"Why not?" He sounded more concerned than he ever did about anything else.

"I think you're right about the children. They really are going to miss me. I'm going to miss them too. I want to see them grow. "

"Tell them to send you some pictures every three months," he joked. "You'll see them grow."

"Robert, this isn't funny," she said indignantly.

"Well, come on. What do you want me to say? Where's all this coming from, anyway? Just yesterday we were talking about all the places we were going to go, all the different people we . . ."

"I'm pregnant Robert!" Dana yelled.

Robert howled and jumped to his feet as if Dana had pounded his chest.

"You're what? How do you figure?"

"I've known for a while because I've been feeling a little weird, but I went to the doctor right after work to make sure . . . and I am definitely with child."

Robert looked at Dana with confusion. As much as she didn't want to admit it, she knew that he was angry with her and with himself, but she couldn't help that. She watched him as he paced the floor shamefully. Was there really anything for him to do now? He paced back and forth and stopped abruptly.

"So what are you going to do?" His words burst out of him.

Dana shot to her feet and screamed, "What do you mean, what am *I* going to do. *We* are going to have a baby!"

"I don't think so. Not if I have anything to do with it! Oh no. You know I don't have time for this now!"

A thick hush filled the room with neither one of them knowing how to break it. Robert stood with his head down while Dana could only stand in anticipation.

Robert whispered, "I'm sorry, Dana. I didn't mean it like that."

"Don't apologize for the truth, Robert" she incensed.

"Come on Dana. You know I would love for us to have a child, but now is not the right time. I have to get my priorities straight first. Everything has to be perfect and in order before I have any more children, you know that. For now, a new baby is just not in the plan."

"Well tell me, what is in the plan *Mr. I'm getting everything perfect and in order*? How long have I heard that you need to get *your* priorities straight? What about *me* Robert?"

Dana couldn't stand to look at his guilty face. She walked across the room in fury and frustration.

"Look, Dana" Robert sympathized. "The plans for the trip are already set."

"Robert! You were planning on taking this trip to Europe with me three years ago. I'm sorry, but it doesn't take that long to plan a trip! You were planning on going with me to visit my parents down south and have you even seen them yet? No! You were planning on giving me back that money I gave you eons ago when your royalty wasn't too royal! And here you are, Mr. Big Time Representative Drake, and I haven't even seen a promissory note! Robert, what about me?"

"Please Dana. You know I'm doing the best I can. This is not exactly an ideal situation," he was calm.

She was fed up with his excuses.

"You know it could've been ideal if you did what you said you were going to do a long time ago."

"So, you planned this huh!"

"No!" Dana shouted. "I didn't plan any of this! None of this!"

Dana's face turned deep red as she now paced the floor. Robert paid her no mind.

"Oh! Don't act up now! This is exactly what you wanted, Ms. Bowman! You want to have my baby so you can show and tell everybody that your beloved child belongs to one of the most powerful black men in the state!"

"Oh shut up and cut the bull!" Dana attacked. "You know I don't care nothing about that!"

"I can see it now across the headlines. 'Representative Drake fathers baby with mistress of eight long years!' And then I'm going to have to think of a way to explain to my wife, my children and the whole county how I even got into this crazy situation!"

"Oh! So now I'm a situation? First, I'm the only woman who can fulfill *all* your desires, and now because I'm pregnant with your baby and I have no desire to kill it, I've automatically turned into a situation! Well, now the situation is, you're gonna be a daddy!"

"You like the sound of that, don't you?" Robert laughed.

Dana was disturbed that he took light of her frustration.

"I knew I couldn't trust you from the first moment I saw you," Robert mocked.

His words pierced Dana's heart like hot fire. How could he say that to her? Ms. Dana Bowman was the only woman he could trust to keep all of his dirty laundry hidden inside her closet. She allowed him to be who he really was in her home, but knew he put on a façade when he walked out into the world. How could he say that when he knew she would keep all of his secrets and bury them with her in the grave? She was hot.

"Don't you date try to blame me for any of this, Robert. You knew from the first moment you saw me, you couldn't trust yourself. You saw me and knew that if you weren't careful, you were gonna get caught in your own trap and you'd cheat on her again! Robert, just face the fact that you have always been, and will always be a dog."

"What!" Robert was shouting.

"Yes, Robert, a d-o-g!" Dana fired back at him. "See, you fail to realize that what this stupid little town sees is nothing compared to what I see every day! Yes, you do have enough money, political power, and charisma to make this whole town of corruption bow down at your feet and make all the politician groupies scream and holler your name. You might have enough royal blood to last you a thousand generations, the finest pedigree in this town. But even a child knows that the finest pedigree, even with the first place gold ribbon wrapped around its neck, still ain't nothing but a dog!"

Dana read him so good; she didn't know how to react. She stood there, staring him down and quite proud of the awesome role she slipped into so easily. "Pretty good for no rehearsal," she thought.

Robert laughed quietly.

"Okay Ms. Bowman. Why don't we cut the whole charade, huh? You just told me that you were pregnant with my child and now you're calling me a dog? I will understand you women." Robert threw up his hands in surrender and sat on the couch. "You women, I tell 'ya."

Dana almost took offense at Robert's indifference, but as she was in her element, she could only look at him in his pitiful state and bust out laughing uncontrollably. She laughed so hard, tears began to form, rolling down the side of her face. But looking at Robert sitting there anxiously waiting for an explanation of her amusement, she made an earnest effort to control her exuberant fit of joy. She wiped her face and tried to retain her dignity.

"Us women huh? We're so fickle. So fickle that you men never know what to expect from *us women*. . .and all this time I thought I was pretty good to you as I waited patiently, with my fickle self, for you, with your perfect self, to get everything in order."

Dana enjoyed herself.

"Look. Obviously this isn't going to be a good night. Why don't you just say what you need to say so I can go home."

"Okay, Robert." Dana used her school teacher voice, "this affair is getting old and you know it. It's time to call it don't you think?"

Robert looked even more confused as he glared at Dana's stomach and questioned her with his eyes.

Dana shook her head. "No Robert, I'm not pregnant," she confessed.

"What? You lied to me?" Robert was demanding as he turned deep red. Dana couldn't tell if he was angry or embarrassed.

"If there was one thing I learned from this *situation*, it was how you would lie just to get a rise out of me. I definitely got one out of you tonight. I see where your heart is and where it has always been. You were never planning on staying with me. Never planned on it." Dana turned away from him, realizing that what she told Robert, she had known all along. He was not the only one to blame. Robert was her fix too.

In his attempt to maintain what was left of his ego, Robert stood in silence and scanned the room. He dared not look at Dana, for he knew that she was not turning back, especially when he spotted his three Gucci suitcases sitting in the corner of the far wall of the living room waiting for him to claim them. Robert froze in doubt as he stared at the suitcases.

Worry started to set in Dana's chest as she gazed a Robert looking just like little Tommy Jenkins standing on the corner of her street, unsure of where to go, or what to do. As much as she wanted to end this episode by picking up those bags for him and throwing him out, her heart did cry out for him. Dana wondered what he was feeling. In that instance, Robert's feelings became more important than her own. Suddenly, flashbacks of their most intimate moments seduced her. Her insides were crying out, pleading for just one more time to be with him. Lord, please just one more time.

Dana's heart was yearning. But her mind, in full control, knew that his healing was not in her hands anymore. Dana could help little Tommy Jenkins, but she couldn't fix this one. Keeping Robert in her life one more day would kill her. All of a sudden, the flashbacks became instant nightmares.

Robert sighed heavily and finally looked at Dana with grief. With his eyes glued to hers, they both knew it was time. Robert nodded slightly and Dana was relieved. The pain in her chest subsided as he walked to the corner, slowly picked up his suitcases and made his way to the stairs. As Robert walked to the garage door, Dana's eyes welled with tears. His shadow against the wall moved dully as he put on his trench coat. He always looked so good in that coat. Dana stared at his shadow that was motionless against the wall and heard him clear his throat as he cautiously walked up the stairs. As soon as Dana was about to shriek at the top of her lungs, he interrupted her attempt.

"What happened to you today, Dana?" He was quiet.

Dana sat on the couch with her head down while the tears fell and suddenly remembered the moment that changed her life. She gazed at the far wall, hypnotized.

"At the end of the day, that little Rashawn came up to me, gave me the biggest hug and said, 'you know what Ms. Bowman. I *love you so much* 'cause you the best teacher in the whole world. How you get to be so smart?'"

Dana managed to grin though she cried her heart out. "When he looked at me and screamed at the top of his lungs, he was so proud. He wasn't at all ashamed to let everybody know how he felt about me. All of a sudden, everything seemed so clear. It felt so good. It *feels* so good."

A warm fire simmered through Dana's body as she closed her eyes to recapture that moment. Suddenly, it seemed that Robert's presence didn't matter to her. She wanted to stay in this moment forever. Robert knew and he respectfully left out of the door into the garage. Dana could hear the sound of his car engine gradually leaving out of her driveway, but she didn't move. The sound became more faint in her ears, and still, she didn't move.

Sitting on the couch, with her arms wrapped around her shoulders, Dana savored this fire that she hungered after for almost ten years. What she thought was unattainable finally was here. As she eagerly sniffed the still fresh aroma of Grandma Mae's cooking, she enjoyed the sweet sounds of Ella. With red, swollen eyes, she looked around her house. She gazed in admiration at the house that she bought with her own money and kept clean with her own hands. Her home. Dana recalled how thrilled she was to decorate and furnish it all by herself when she moved in ten years ago. She told all her girlfriends to come see her new place. She was proud. Yes. Dana was proud of her home, and as she sat still meditating on that memory alone. She took in a deep breath, allowing the memory to make itself permanent in her heart.

Yes. Ms. Dana Bowman finally made her move and it was time to celebrate. She wiped her face dry, grabbed the stereo remote, turned up Ella full blast and hurried to the kitchen to make her own plate of Grandma Mae's jerk chicken, spiced greens and sweet cornbread. Dana poured herself a glass of freshly squeezed lemonade, set herself down at her own table, blessed her food, thanked the Lord for Rashawn, and with deepest humility, enjoyed her house-warming party.

Penda L. James

DANDELION BOUQUETS

Most people don't give a damn about dandelions. I hated them when I was growing up! I used to pop their heads off and throw them into the street. I plucked them to make bouquets that lasted only twenty minutes. As kids we trampled them under our feet, kicked them and cut them with scissors just for fun.

Was I permanently damaged?

Like most people, I didn't understand the significance of dandelions. I recall from yard work that the roots were difficult to extract. I worked so hard that my clothes would be drenched with sweat. Sometimes I would have to use tools to dig up the root. Not only that, my arms would hurt and my fingers bled from the resistance of its *Lion's Tooth* leaves against my skin. When I finally plucked one from the ground, I would hold it above my head like a trophy of my victory. It felt good to finally feel the root release from the ground.

No one saw him pulling my hair out by the follicles, or squeezing my budding breasts until the bruises turned blood red. They saw what they wanted to see, believed what they wanted to believe about me.

His lies created a distorted image of me to the other kids in the neighborhood. By the time I was in sixth grade, I had no friends I could trust. They snickered, pointed their fingers at me, and judged me. They never knew the scars he was etching on my soul.

I wanted to tell them the truth, my truth, but his version was so much more intriguing to them. "That's why she don't have no teeth you know. . ."

As you can imagine, with my contempt for dandelions, it was to my chagrin when my father admonished me, "Be a dandelion Pen."

That which you resist will persist.
–Dr. Clayton Grisby

"Huh?" If he could have seen my facial expression . . .

"If you are like a tulip, you'll be beautiful for two weeks and then you'll be dead. If you are a dandelion, your roots are strong, and you have longevity."

"Dad. . ."

He didn't hear my protest, "Dandelions can grow anywhere. They dig their roots in deep and their babies pop up all over. That's how you want to be, baby."

I'm thankful for that conversation with my Daddy, but I wish it had come much sooner in my life.

> *I was only seven. What could my little body possibly have given to that eighteen year old man?*

> *I remember him holding me by my throat against the house in the dark backyard so he could have his way with me. I remember that I wanted to watch Benji and eat popcorn with his sister and brother while my parents entertained their friends in the living room. I remember my mother looking for me, calling my name. With his hands on my throat, I couldn't answer her.*

Unbeknownst to me, the things I did to dandelions affected them only on the surface. The flowers may have been mutilated, but the root was always untouched. Dandelions have many uses. If made into tea and consumed, they can cleanse the liver. If eaten in a salad, dandelions can supplement potassium and other vitamins in the body. Bees cultivate the nectar and pollen of these flowers and produce honey. Dandelions are even known to help people relieve stress. It makes sense to me now that if you don't uproot and destroy the entire core, the only thing the dandelion can do is grow back. That's the lesson my father wanted me to learn.

I knew he didn't really like me, but then, I didn't really like myself yet. I was only in sixth grade. What did I know about anything other than jumping rope, drinking Hawaiian Punch and getting my hair braided? On that day, he didn't come bearing gifts like he usually did, he just decided that he would take what he wanted from me . . .

So when he grabbed my broom, taking and then demanding something for nothing, something inside of me clicked. How dare he interrupt my concert with Bobby Brown! I was minding my own business and he had no right to enter my personal space. In that moment that he took my broom, he turned on a switch in my mind that woke me up. I was tired of being his punching bag. I was tired of being a victim in every circumstance. I snapped.

He ran home with my broom and I was dead on his heels. I jumped down the steps of my house, ran between the bushes and jumped through the fence gate as he tried to close it on my leg. He ran up the steps and I was right behind him wanting to kill. What I didn't know was that it was a set up!

As we stood on his porch fighting, his cousins were in the house waiting for the right moment to push the door open and pull me inside. Thinking back, we must have been the only four people on the street at the time. No one was outside and no one saw anything happen.

I put up a good fight. I punched him in the jaw, kicked him in the groin and tried to run back home, but he was bigger, stronger and more devious than me. His cousins grabbed me, covered my mouth so I couldn't scream and dragged me by my hair upstairs to him where he had run ahead waiting for me . . .

I remember hearing them laughing at me as I staggered home with a bleeding vagina, sore legs, arms and throat. Not only had they set me up against my will, they pushed me out of a third story window when he was finished so they wouldn't get caught by his mother! I remember the pain in my breasts and I remember the anger and contempt I felt toward myself for allowing myself to be victimized. Again.

That was the last time.

Although I thought for years that I was completely healed from sexual abuse that started when I was seven, the truth is, the residue from that experience has been a thread in my existence. Unlike the dandelion root, this weed in my heart was not beneficial to me. Its thick roots choked my desire to look good. For years I hid behind hats, big jeans and baggy t-shirts, dressing very unattractively, homely even. Now I am fighting to release extra pounds which replaced the big clothes.

This poison flowed into the perception that I have the responsibility of always keeping peace in the midst of conflict. I tried to buy love just like I was bought with Hawaiian Punch and candy. Not only that, I have chosen low-paying jobs that don't compensate me for my skills, experience or education. Then I turn around and complain that I never have enough money.

My view of friendships has also been distorted. I chose to hang around people who distracted me from my goals, but I helped them achieve theirs. I saw so many people pass me by that I often wondered if my dreams would ever become reality. I didn't think I deserved anything good so I became the scapegoat for everyone else's problems.

Even my relationship with my father was effected by this experience. For a long time I feared my daddy, avoided conversation and evaded being in his presence. In some ways, back then I saw him as just like them — the men who stole from me. *Daddy won't understand, he's a man too.* But thankfully, as I have matured and released my brokenness, my eyes have been opened to the unconditional love of my father. I am now able to find the protection and solace I needed then, in the comfort of his wisdom.

Well, I have asked myself, why should I cover these beautiful wings?

"You are stronger than you think you are. . ."
–Joi Horton

If I were a tulip, I would have been long gone. I am determined not to allow my past to have power over my future; its influence must only be for my good. Trying to ignore that things transpired doesn't change the fact that they happened. Yes, I was sexually abused, but those experiences are only one part of my composition as a woman. Despite the fact that I ripped the pages of my journals to erase that damaged girl from my mind, she exists in my memory. She won't let me forget her, I am because she is.

> *They saw me exposed. There were people in the neighborhood who walked by us in the field and in the alley. They peeked through the door in his bedroom where he had dragged me against my will. They stood in the garage and watched as he plucked at my leaves, but they never saw my value.*

Taking my lesson from dandelions, I will recognize that I have been misinterpreted as meaningless, but my value is far above rubies. Like my daddy told me, I will dig my roots in deep to stake my claim on the ground where I stand. I am stronger, wiser and call me victim no more! There has always been something in me that stirred me to survive when I didn't think I had the strength.

Thank God for those stubborn roots. The roots of the dandelion in me helped me survive.

> *When you embrace*
> *all that you are*
> *And release everything that*
> *you don't need to be*
> *You'll be free.*

Today, I will find some dandelions. I will be gentle as I grasp them in my hands and make a bouquet. To remember, and to forget.

GATHERING THE WISDOM FROM FREE TO FLY

"Therefore I take pleasure in infirmities, in reproaches, in necessities, in persecutions, in distresses for Christ's sake:
for when I am weak, then am I strong."
(II Corinthians 12:10)

Going through painful situations and circumstances is not easy, but it is part of living. Challenges are endurable when we know our lives are hid in Christ and He is there for us no matter what happens.

It is a testament of God's love, grace, and mercy when we overcome painful experiences in our lives. When we are honest and open to share them with others, we remind them that they are not alone and that God will not forget them in their pain . . . if they will allow Him the space and place in their hearts and lives.

People often misquote the Bible by saying, "and the truth shall set you free." Jesus says, "And ye shall know the truth, and the truth shall make you free." (John 8:32) Condemnation and shame will cause us to edit painful pasts and presents, but your freedom is tied to your being free from baggage from your past or present. Knowing the truth is not enough to liberate you. Choosing to know and allowing the truth to work on the inside of you (not condemnation, hate, wrath, rage, etc) to bring you closer to Jesus will bring you freedom.

1. Have you shared your testimony? If you have not shared your testimony, find someone (a sister, a cousin, a daughter, etc.) to share your story with so that they too will know freedom.

2. What do you think about each of the four seasons that have been discussed throughout this book? Describe a situation in your life that has taken you through all four seasons.

The strength of a woman is . . .

her unwavering faith in God.
Teri Miller Barker

her silence.
Gerald Lee Fisher

love.
Joi L. Horton

her resilience and hope.
Penda L. James

her confidence.
Cheryl Vasser

found when she is being true to herself.
A. Sheri Wise

THE CONTRIBUTORS

TIWANDA ALSTON resides in Pittsburgh, PA where she enjoys being a mother, creating greeting cards, gift journals and poetry. She is currently working on her memoir, <u>He Held Me Close: Real Accounts of a Life Almost Lost.</u>

CHRISTINE ARNETT lives in the Louisville, KY area. She is a preschool teacher with an incredible family – a loving husband and two amazing children.

KENYA ARNOLD is a graduate of Wilberforce University. She enjoys serving the Lord and is a member of Sigma Gamma Rho Sorority.

LENA ARNOLD is the author of *For This Child We Prayed: Living with the Secret Shame of Infertility and For This Dream We Prayed Companion Journal.* Lena and her husband Horace started *IN*fertility Press an imprint of Emperor Publishing, in an effort to dispel many of the myths associated with infertility in both the African-American and Christian communities.

AVALYN*ABIJAH** rediscovered her first love, Jesus Christ and in doing so, was set free to write that others may be spiritually liberated thru her testimonies. In seeking her life's purpose she found that it all about God and His purpose for her life. Saved from distraction after distraction – she ultimately found her way back to Him and became "free to fly!" Auntie, writer, lawyer, mentor, encourager, presently residing in Toledo, Ohio. *[worshiper of Jehovah]*

TERI MILLER BARKER is a freelance writer who has written for television, radio, newspapers, and national magazines. Her powerful, positive, and uplifting essays and articles have provided inspiration to many, and can be read on her website, www.thewriteawaycafe.com. Mrs. Barker, an alumna of Wilberforce University, resides in Dayton, Ohio with her husband and daughter.

TERYN ALIYA BARKER is a talented and outspoken ten year old who is in the fifth grade. In addition to modeling and acting, Teryn is an A-student who enjoys swimming, bike riding, playing piano and writing poetry.

DANADA BECKWITH recalls writing as far back as the sixth grade. She is working on her book The Little Girl in Me Wouldn't Let Me Be a Woman. Danada is the proud mother of two athletic boys and resides in Dayton, OH.

Free to Fly is the second anthology for freelance writer EBONY BROUSSARD who has won several writing contests. She is currently working on another anthology project and a children's book. Ebony is grateful for the support of her husband and her daughter and the inspiration of the Holy Spirit.

GWENDOLYN BUCHANAN's mission is to inspire and empower girls and women to discover, embrace and manifest their divine potential. A certified Rites of Passage facilitator and Family

Development Specialist, Gwen has recently begun to allow the songs in her heart to sing through her writing. Gwen is a mother of three and a grand-mother of two.

THERESA A. BURRAGE studied creative writing at Lancaster University in England. Theresa, a Wilberforce University Graduate has poetry published in numerous publications. Theresa is currently working on a book of poetry which will reflect on love, life and relationships. You can find her gospel rap/poetry CD, *Lyrics for the Soul* at www.cdbaby.com.

SHANTAL "PEACHES" CABELL resides in East Pittsburgh, PA. She and her husband Baker are proud parents of two beautiful daughters, Bakisha and Alexis. Although Peaches is originally from Kentucky, she is a devoted Pittsburgh Steelers fan. Shantal is a comedienne who has performed at various comedy events around the country.

TANIKA M. CARWILE was born and raised in Baltimore, MD. "Tee Tee" is a Claims Representative for the Social Security Administration. A dedicated member of the Soul Harvest Church and Ministries where Min. Merrill R. Griffin is her pastor she serves as the Church Clerk, President of the Usher's Ministry, and Youth Advisor.

CATT4297 lives with her mother in Pittsburgh, PA. She is open-minded and enjoys writing.

TYRHONDA COLEMAN is a community outreach educator and founder of Mary James Helping Hands of Dayton, a teaching ministry and support service organization. TyRhonda has a Bachelors of Science Degree in Human Services and is a 2nd year graduate student in Psychology.

NICOLE L. COLVIN graduated from Wilberforce University. She earned an MBA from Tiffin University and her Masters of Divinity from Ashland Theological Seminary with a focus in Women's Studies. Pastor Nicole has preached, taught, and conducted workshops around the country. She is a member of Alpha Kappa Alpha Sorority, Inc and is married to Reverend Nathaniel Colvin, III.

DIANE DANIELS and her husband James Sales live in Pittsburgh, PA. She has operated DID & Associates, a multi-faceted public relations firm since 1983. This is her first entry in an anthology, but as a journalist she has written countless news articles throughout her career. Contact Diane at: www.didassociates.net or e-mail: diane@didassociates.net

STEPHANIE DAVIS is a native of Baltimore, MD. She enjoys meeting new people, taking pictures and working with individuals who have special needs. She likes to think outside of the box and looks for opportunities to expand her life and well-being.

TEISHA DURHAM is a native of Dayton, OH. She has volunteered for several organizations including hospitals, homeless shelters and a local publishing company. In addition to trying to help inspire young people to use their gifts and talents to rise above their circumstances and help others, Teisha consistently strives to find ways to transform her community.

ORIENTA NICOLE EISON graduated from the University of Cincinnati with a degree in African American Studies. She obtained her Master of Arts in Counseling from Xavier University. Orienta enjoys working with children as a licensed professional counselor/ mental health therapist.

SELENER FIELDS was deeply loved by her family. A graduate of Wilberforce University, Selener was constantly in pursuit of her dreams until her passing. As part of her legacy, she encouraged those she loved to accomplish their goals.

LASHONDA B. FULLER LSC, LLPC earned her Bachelors of Science in Journalism, Masters of Education in Guidance & Counseling from Bowling Green State University, and is currently pursuing her Ph.D. in Counselor Education at Western Michigan University. Writing has served as an avenue to express her experience since she was a teenager raised in the inner city of Detroit.

JUDI GAZAWAY resides with her family in Cincinnati, Ohio.

MAYA DANIELLE GREEN is a Process Improvement Analyst for the Florida Department of Management Services. She earned her B.S. in Industrial and Operations Engineering from The

University of Michigan. Maya has lost a total of 102 lbs through prayer, eating healthy, and becoming physically active. Her ultimate goal is to lose 150 lbs and become a fitness and wellness coach.

MYRA MICHELE GEORGE lives in Columbus, Ohio. She shares her life with her husband and best friend, Pastor Ronald A. George and their sons, Joshua and Jordan. A graduate of Hampton University and Clemson University, Chele is a researcher working as a Pharmaceutical Sales Representative. She is a personal trainer and a self proclaimed natural hairstylist.

CHARLENE A. HILL-ELLISON holds a Masters Degree in Organizational Leadership. An associate minister at Mt. Ararat Baptist Church and mother of two, she is involved in many community activities that mentor and build leadership in youth. Charlene recently founded The SEAL (Self Empowerment Actualization/Acceptance and Love) Program, a program of empowerment, self-discovery, self-worth, self-esteem, value, and purpose.

MARLA HOLLOWAY desires to do the perfect will of God. Through her writing God is delivering her and she desires to share the same with others. Marla resides in the wonderful city of Dayton, Ohio with her family where she and her husband Co-Pastor Kingdom Life Christian Center. (P.O. Box 6, Dayton, Ohio 45405, (937) 830-6817 or peachesholloway1@aol.com).

CONI HOOKFIN is a wife and mother of two wonderful children. Her goal is to pursue higher education and a higher glory that she will use to motivate, strengthen and uplift broken communities worldwide.

MARILYN JOY PITTS HORTON shares her life with her husband of 33 years, Will. She is mother of four and has two precious grandchildren, Elijah and Amaris. Marilyn is thankful for second chances to experience joy, live with hope and walk with focus.

SYLVIA JEWETT has been writing poetry and short stories for over thirty five years. Known today as the family poet, she writes for special occasions and family gatherings. Free to Fly is her first published work. Ms. Jewett is a mother of three and resides in Dayton, Ohio.

JAQUAN JOHNSON discovered her creative imagination at an early age. Jaquan's first play, *A Good Girl's Cry* was written in 2001. Her second stage play, *Husband and Wives* was penned in 2003. Jaquan has in the process of publishing her first book, <u>Lord Deliver Me from These BIG Girl Blues.</u>

Rev. ANNIE M. WRIGHT JONES is married to Minister Al Jones of Al Jones Entrepreneurial Consultants. They have five children and 11 grand-children and currently reside in Charlotte, NC. Anne is the founder of Sisters Achieving Safety and Sanctity through Yoke-Breaking Ministry (S.A.S.S.Y) *God's daughter. Purposely walking in faith.*

VALERIE D. JONES, third of five children was born in Milwaukee, WI but was raised in Dayton, Ohio. Moving to Mississippi and enduring years of an abusive marriage, she divorced and returned to Ohio. Today she is remarried, the mother of five, a grandmother of seven grandchildren, minister of the Gospel and a rising author.

A southern belle at heart, LAUREN LAKE spent her childhood and adolescence in Birmingham, Alabama. She later went on to pursue a Bachelors degree in Graphic Design with a concentration in Magazine Production from Florida A&M University. Lauren continues to travel and pursue her passions while being sensitive to God's direction.

LIZBETH FIGUEROA MARINO was born and raised in Puerto Rico. After having the opportunity to intern at Walt Disney World where she eventually met her husband. Lizbeth obtained her Masters Degree in Business Administration in Aviation from Embry-Riddle Aeronautical University in California. Today she resides with her spouse and daughter in Virginia.

LYNETTE MICHELLE MASHIRI is a poet with much to say. She is now letting go of the veil to let the world hear them. Words are an expression of the soul and how we use them matters. Lynette hopes to touch someone with the order of words she uses.

YOLANDA MCELROY currently lives in Columbus, Ohio where she seeks to serve God.

TINA RENEE MCKINNEY is a pseudonym for Lena Marie Arnold. Her best friends during high school inspired this piece and the pseudonym is a combination of their names. It is dedicated to the W. 2nd Crew. You know who you are!

JOYCE NELSON and her husband of thirty-eight years live in Wilkinsburg, Pennsylvania. She is the proud mother of one daughter and three step-children. Joyce loves to read and write and up until recently she had limited her writing to family and friends. Joyce loves the Lord and her church and is blessed by serving others.

SHANNA OWENS resides in Cincinnati, Ohio with her family. She enjoys spending time with her four children.

KARASIMONE PENNYBAKER and her husband Nathaniel have a son, Jonathan. Karasimone enjoys singing, serving in her church and being an example of worship. She and her family call Pittsburgh home.

SIERRA LEONE, born Lucy Armstrong, is from Toledo, Ohio. She earned a Masters of Art in Applied Behavioral Science from Wright State University. Sierra has shared the stage with names such as The Last Poets, Nikki Giovanni, Lyfe Jennings, Sonia Sanchez, Amiri Baraka, Haki Madhubuti, Saul Williams, Georgia Me, Tommy Bottoms, Jessica Care-Moore, & others. She is a poet, author, community activist, and entrepreneur.

LYNDELL OCTAVIA ROBINSON was born in the small town of Indianola in the Mississippi Delta. She fell in love with writing at a very young age. Before she found her audible voice, God allowed her to find solace and strength in the written word. She now shares her passion for writing through New Life Deliverance Ministries in Lawrenceville, Georgia.

LAFLORA SHOLAR has been writing since the age of ten. She has written religious plays, screenplays, short stories and many poems. In September 2002 she met Mitchell Sholar on a cruise to Aruba and they married three months later. An alumnus of Roosevelt University, LaFlora lives in Chicago.

ALVINA D. SMITH enjoys letting people know that there is greatness in them. Life's experiences have taught her that she can do nothing without God who has done all things for us in Christ Jesus. Her favorite scripture is Jeremiah 29:11.

ROBIN TAYLOR is a graduate of Wilberforce University. She is a native of Dayton, Ohio and currently resides in Conyers, Georgia with her daughter Taylor.

DENISE THOMAS is a well respected labor coach and childbirth education in Dayton, Ohio. She is wise in areas including preparing for college, starting a business and mothering women. God has given her a wonderful husband and four children including twins. She can be reached at beneeh@att.net.

PAISHA THOMAS is in the training and development field. She has many gifts including poetry, singing, Spanish, and painting. Paisha resides in Columbus, Ohio with her family.

uNique (NAN-C LYNN MOSS) is the only daughter of Martha Ann O'Bannon Moss and the late Aron Moss, Jr. She is the coolest aunt to Za'Vaughn, McKenze and Zion Moss! She is a proud graduate of Wright State University where she earned a Master's Degree in Public Administration. She currently serves her Alma Mater as the Director of Development for the College of Liberal Arts.

MARIAMA WHYTE is a writer, performer, songwriter and actress from Cleveland, Ohio. After touring with the Broadway national tour of "The Color Purple" where she played Celie, Nettie and in the female ensemble, Mariama returned home to write and record her album, "On the Run" which is soon to be released.

KRISTIN M. YOUNG a native of Baltimore, Maryland is currently pursuing her Master's degree in Counseling Psychology at Bowie State University. An active member of Set the Captives Free Outreach Center, in Woodlawn, Maryland. Kristin has a passion for helping others and has been writing spiritual inspirations since 2006. Kristin has been happily married to her gift from God, Mr. James Young since September 2008.

ABOUT THE EDITOR

Put the pen in your hand and let your heart speak.
Your thoughts are bound, yearning to be free. . .
INSPIRE others,
INSCRIBE your words in stone;
Cut deep, heal, and restore.
Put the pen in your hand let it be . . .

Penda L. James is a proud graduate of Wilberforce University and Bowling Green State University. Through her publishing company, InSCRIBEd Inspiration she fuels her passion to help writers achieve their goals. Penda spends her spare time reading, writing or watching movies. She lives in Pittsburgh with her husband and daughter where she is working on her first novel, a handbook for mothers who have children with food allergies and a book about youth pastors and their wives.

ACKNOWLEDGEMENTS:

*For relationships that were lost because of
things that were said, (and never said),
for brokenness that came after decisions that
were made.
for conquered fears and those still taunting us,
for time spent learning to stand tall again*

*we are thankful for the freedom to fly above our
circumstances on wings of faith. . .*

I am humbled by the outpouring of support I received for this project. The contributors trusted me with their writing – you helped me birth a vision that I have been carrying for nine years! Thank you for your patience!

Dawnese Mahaffey designed the butterfly. Wanda Hill reminded me that <u>Free to Fly</u> was not dead, even after it was buried in my heart! Lauren Lake extended herself beyond her limits to contribute the graphic design. Stephanie "Sparkle" Davis, thank you for your photographic eye.

My reader's group – your input was necessary for strengthening this work:
- Lena Arnold (thank you for the years of your example, your sisterhood and your faith in me),
- Teri Miller Barker (your spirit of excellence is appreciated),

- Robin Evans (Wilberforce in the house!)
- Ebony Broussard thank you for writing **Gathering the Wisdom** — your questions over the years have nurtured my growth.
- Avalyn Pitts (my Aunt Avie, you have always believed in me, thank your for encouraging me to keep writing).

Finally, to the strength in my bloodline, Thanks mommy and daddy for welcoming me home whenever I feel broken. My siblings — I stand on your shoulders; you are the legs that keep me standing tall.

Go. . . Make Disciples:
Nuggets for your journey

Rev. Annie Jones, Author

"...For God so loved the world that He gave His only begotten Son, that who ever believes in Him should not perish, but have eternal life..."
John 3:16

This unique workbook is full of journal exercises and Biblical teachings that will assist you in recording your thoughts, reflections and prayers of your experiences on the mission field of daily life. Contemplate the nuggets of wisdom, consider the words of Christ, and put into practice His teachings as you make disciples with your lifestyle and example.

Rev. Jones is the founder of S.A.S.S.Y. (Sisters Achieving Safety and Sanctity through Yoke-breaking) Ministry. Annie develops Biblical curricula, trains Bible Study teachers, designs and implements women's ministry programs, and develops training workshops for Praise Teams and choirs.

God's Daughter. Purposely Walking In Faith.

Spring, 2010

Strong Black Coffee: Poetry and Prose to Encourage, Enlighten, and Entertain Americans of African Descent

Retail Price: $12.95
ISBN-13: 978-0979561337
Available on Amazon.com

www.strongblackcoffee.info
Ask for it at your local bookstore!

Inspired to be...

The inner strength of women that causes them to stand with confidence when their wings have been broken is beautiful. *Free to fly: Wisdom for the Seasons in a Woman's Life* is a celebration of this strength. The contributors to this collection have opened their hearts to expose you to experiences that could have broken them, yet they emerged *Free to Fly* with a testimony. These writings will provoke discussion, inspire you to dream & encourage you to ponder your own freedom. Pre-order your copy today!

ORDER FORM

PRICE	TAX	QUANTITY	TOTAL AMOUNT
$14.95	($1.05) Included		

☐ My check or money order in the amount
$_____ is enclosed.

SUBTOTAL	
SHIPPING $3.00 per book	
GRAND TOTAL	

Direct checks or inquiries to:
InSCRIBEd Inspiration, LLC.
Attention: Penda L. James
P.O. Box 8778
Pittsburgh, PA 15221
(937) 554-4636
PlJames_scribe@yahoo.com

Name _____
Mailing Address _____
City/State/Zip _____
Phone (____) _____
Email _____